# Manag
# the
# Enabling Authority

by

## Rodney Brooke

General Editors: Michael Clarke and John Stewart

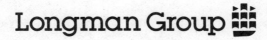

Longman Group

in association with the Local Government Training Board

Published by Longman Group UK Limited
Longman House, Burnt Mill, Harlow, Essex CM20 2JE

First published 1989

**British Library Cataloguing in Publication Data**
Brooke, Rodney
  GTB: managing beyond the local authority.
  1. Great Britain. Local authorities. Management
  I. Title
  352.41

ISBN 0-582-04090-6

Typeset by Page Bros (Norwich) Ltd
Printed in Great Britain by Bell and Bain Ltd., Glasgow

# Contents

# Other titles in the series

# Preface

Local authorities have a general commitment to the welfare of their areas which extends beyond their statutory functions. This long-standing concern has recently become encapsulated in the phrase, 'the enabling authority'. Its full implementation will have the most profound effect on local authority organisation and management. As well as implying a general concern to affect external agencies, the phrase also reflects contraction in the role of local authorities as direct providers of services. In some cases this is through statute: transport, airports, compulsory competitive tendering, education, housing. In other cases local authorities themselves are embracing the concept with enthusiasm. It is, of course, easy to exaggerate this trend. In the immediate future local authorities will continue to be major direct providers.

Nevertheless a whole new vocabulary is being introduced into the world of local government. Phrases like 'the management of influence' and 'the conduit for local choice' are bandied around. The concept of the enabling authority spans the political spectrum. Some see the diminution of municipal empires as a good in itself. Others see the attraction of ending the pre-occupation with the management of direct services. Some see the local authority's residual role as being minimal. Others see it enlarged as the authority frees itself from the administration of its own services to look at the wider needs of the community. But all local authorities will continue to wish to affect at least some services they do not provide directly, whether it be the closing of a sub-post office, the removal of a telephone box or the stimulation of the local economy.

While the idea of the enabling authority is surrounded by polemic, there is remarkably little thought as to how exactly an enabling authority can be managed. What canvas should it choose? What mechanisms can it use? What skills will it require? What will the role of councillors be when they are free from the burden of direct provision? This book seeks to answer these questions and to provide a practical handbook of use to councillors, officers and all with an interest in the development of the enabling authority. It is principally structured round the different relationships between the local authority and the external agencies and how those relationships can be managed. The first chapter sets in context the development of the enabling authority. The second identifies the role of the enabling authority and how it can operate. The remaining chapters identify ways in which the local authority can be effective within the different relationships it establishes.

There is a certain amount of academic research available in some areas, e.g. joint working between local authorities, joint community care schemes and the intervention of the local authority in the local economy. On the whole there is a considerable lack of documented experience and certainly no manual

of advice. This book is the first of its kind. Since many of its concepts are
relatively undeveloped, I have not hesitated to illustrate it by example when-
ever possible. I make no apologies for drawing heavily on my own experience,
partial though it may be. I hope that memory has not played me false, but if
my examples are inaccurate I hope that they are at least *ben trovato*.

In order to avoid unnecessary words, I have occasionally used the word
'he'. Could I make it clear that, like all lawyers, I intend the word to include
the feminine wherever that is appropriate.

I owe a great debt to a number of people who have taken much time and
trouble to discuss the topic with me. A list of acknowledgements is necessarily
incomplete, but may I single out Simon Baddeley and Professor Ken Young
from the Institute of Local Government Studies, University of Birmingham;
Norman Flynn of the London Business School; Professor George Jones and
Tony Travers of the London School of Economics. Steve Leach of INLOGOV
and Dr David Hunter of the Nuffield Institute for Health Service Studies,
the University of Leeds, both went to extraordinary lengths not only to
discuss the issues with me but also to provide me with published and
unpublished manuscripts which were extremely helpful.

The editors of the series have made a great contribution not only to local
government but also to this book. Michael Clarke played a great part in
helping me to structure a mass of inchoate ideas by suggesting the basic
framework. My debt to Professor John Stewart of INLOGOV extends well
beyond the confines of this volume. His input to the ideas of local government
over two decades has substantially changed its concept and practice. The
quality of thinking has been immeasurably improved by the series of booklets
which he and Michael Clarke have issued over the last few years. The
manuscript has benefitted from comments from both editors, David Hunter
and Steve Leach, and from my colleagues Matthew Ives and Helen Moss.

The select bibliography at the end of the book is partly an invitation to
further reading but is also an acknowledgement of other debts.

January 1989

## Acknowledgements

We gratefully acknowledge permission to reproduce extracts from the follow-
ing: City of Bradford, *The Changing Face of Bradford 1984*. Hansard, *Hansard*
(14th December 1987). Local Government Training Board, *Councillors and
Competition 1988*. HMSO, *The Conduct of Local Authority Business 1988*.
Newcastle City Council, *Grey Street Renaissance*. LGTB, *Managing Tomorrow
1988*. Home Office, *Working Party on 1987*. Community Trust Development,
*Community Trust Handbook*, 2nd ed., 1987. City of Westminster, *Licensing
Objections*.

# 1   Introduction

## The rise and fall of the corporate local authority

The medieval municipal corporation was a corporate body. So (in legal terms) are its statutory successors. Yet by the middle of the twentieth century local authorities were regarded and run more as a congeries of separate services than as corporate entities.

Partly this was due to the way in which services had been added to and subtracted from local authority control from the nineteenth century reforms onwards. They were taken on and transferred as self-contained concerns. More important was the way the local authorities ran their own affairs. Committees followed the boundaries of professional departments. Each Chairman had 'his' or 'her' Chief Officer and department.

In 1966 an Education Committee decided to introduce paper crockery into its schools meals service. This would save the Education Department £10 000 per annum. Audit scrutiny showed that the change would cost the Cleansing Department £50 000 per annum extra. The Education Committee were not deterred by this corporate loss. Eventually the full Council, voting across party lines, overruled the Committee – the only mechanism for subordinating the departmental interest to the corporate good.

The multiplicity of committees and departments defied central co-ordination and planning. In any case there was no central mechanism either politically or administratively. Policy Committees did not exist and the mechanism for political co-ordination was through the budget only. The Clerk was 'primus inter pares', only first among equals. Government Departments parallelled professional departments and related directly to them.

In the 1960s this attitude changed fundamentally. There was pressure for local authorities to be managed from a corporate centre, an impetus originally developed from the need to sort out information technology requirements and priorities for the new computers which were augmenting the Treasurers' adding machines. Town Clerks developed a new role and began to be styled Chief Executives. Politicisation threw up Leaders who saw a role beyond presiding over the allocation of the annual budget. The Leaders and Chief Executives complemented each other's interests in the corporate nature of the local authority. Party groups homogenised. Corporate administrative structures were created.

During the 1960s planning was a powerful tool for shaping communities as it responded to both demographic and economic growth. Growth provided an impetus to strategic planning which could be exercised through development control. At a time of full employment pressures for unacceptable developments could be resisted. Planners developed new corporate inspirations and a vision for strategic planning reflected in the Planning Advisory Group Report of 1965.

The professional solutions of charismatic Chief Officers began to seem either undesirable or infeasible or both. Town centre redevelopments, urban motorways and high rise blocks were disliked. It became clear that residential care for the elderly as a blanket solution was neither desirable nor economically possible. Society itself changed the problems of the local authorities. Professions structured around the old problems were no longer able to provide single professional solutions to the new. Public challenge prompted greater thought about the nature of services.

Widely accepted reports like Mallaby on Local Government Staffing (1966) and Maud on Local Government Management (1967) prompted corporate thinking. Their recommendations included drastic reductions in the number of committees and departments, simplifying the practicalities of corporate management. The Ministry of Housing and Local Government became the Department of the Environment, giving a national imprimatur to the changed nature of local authorities.

Policy planning systems sprung up to provide a framework for the new central concept of management. Budgets were seen as misleading pieces of management information. Programme budgets sprang up. Questions were asked about the purpose for which services were provided.

Once problems were defined corporately then solutions could be corporately adopted. The Housing Department's problems on vandalism might be solved by the Engineer's Departments installing better street lighting. Reports such as the Plowden report on Primary Education (1967) saw the interconnection between services. The best way to improve educational standards might in practice be to spend money on housing.

The National Associations of Local Authorities had organised themselves in the same way as their constituents and government departments, service by service. But in the 1960s new institutions started to address the issues of local government as a whole. The Local Government Training Board had a remit across all aspects of local government. The Institute of Local Government Studies at Birmingham University needed an academic rationale for English Local Government and naturally came up with a corporate answer.

By the 1970s political leaders and groups, Chief Executives and academic bodies all had a vested interest in developing the corporate nature of local government. New public relations departments responded to and further developed corporatism. Local authorities were presented to their residents as corporate entities as house styles were developed and a corporate message relayed. Corporatism was heady wine. Those who drunk deep at the Pierian spring realised that they had a powerful instrument at their disposal. As well as responding to the changing needs of society, a local authority could change society itself through the combined exercise of its policies. A more systematic approach to policy planning prompted multi-departmental solutions to issues.

Local authorities examined facilities provided to their communities.

When viewed across departmental boundaries it became obvious that expensive facilities in schools were capable of community use out of school hours with only relatively minor modifications. Entrenched opposition by education departments and head teachers changed to enthusiastic acceptance by the education establishment of the concept of community schools.

The County Boroughs were the leaders in these developments. They combined a wide range of powers with a closeness to their communities, political control with a tradition of innovative thinking, multi-dimensional problems with a willingness to spend money. The apotheosis of the new corporatism came with the publication in 1969 of the Redcliffe–Maud Report on the Reorganisation of Local Government. The County Borough writ large was to be the model for local government everywhere. The exciting new world of corporatism could be explored throughout the country in a series of unitary authorities. The nexus between the different services was the major rationale of Redcliffe–Maud. The report encapsulated the conventional wisdom of the day.

The rational managerial approach of the Report did not, however, fit political realities or topographical loyalties. The hopes of the new corporate thinkers were shattered into four fragments. The solution adopted by the Government in its response to Redcliffe–Maud did not provide unified local government throughout the country. Instead it chose the reverse solution, by dividing the powers of the County Boroughs between County Councils, District Councils, Water Authorities and Health Authorities. County areas shared the same structures.

At the same time the collapse of the post-war boom undermined the effectiveness of the planning process. The new structure planning process proved too vague to be effective as a strategic process when not underpinned by growth. Unemployment prompted departures from strategic policies.

The new corporate planning processes proved bureaucratic, unwieldy and unsuited to the political process. Management time was perforce diverted to the disruption of reorganisation, the creation of the new authorities and a long period of declining resources.

The corporate local authority had disappeared just as it was getting into its stride.

## 1974 and after: the inter-corporate renaissance

Of course the County Borough of the 1960s was not an island. It was not self-contained in its powers. Nor did it carry out its functions exclusively by use of its own staff: contractors have always been used by local authorities. It interacted with the private sector in its own area and with local unions.

The voluntary sector, though less important then both as political force and as provider of services, was nevertheless influential in any locality. Some voluntary organisations, like the Council for the Preservation of Rural England and the National Trust, had national status as lobbyers. Statutory quangos, like the Forestry Commission, the Countryside Commission and the Arts Council, wielded great influence in their spheres.

The occasional private water and cemetery companies survived from the nineteenth century. Statutory Undertakers, in many areas assuming functions formerly exercised by the local authorities, were a crucial part of the provision of local services. The Council had to interact with Government Departments, the Departments of the Environment, Transport and Health and Social Security, the Home Office, both financially and for operational purposes.

Moreover, through a combination of economics, ecology, practicality and Government pressure the Boroughs had to surrender parts of their services to joint operation: sewage disposal, refuse disposal, children's homes regional planning, higher education. Regional development and tourist associations sprang up voluntarily as local authorities recognised the limitations of their own geographical boundaries and finances.

The 1960s saw portents of things to come. All save the largest authorities lost their police forces to regional groupings as motorways destroyed the insular pattern of crime. Metropolitan-wide passenger transport authorities were set up to take over the newly loss-making municipal bus fleets. A national drought precipitated the formation of multi-authority water boards.

The experience of Stockport was typical. Faced with an unprecedented drought the construction of a new reservoir became imperative. No loan sanction was forthcoming unless the County Borough shared its resources with neighbouring authorities through the medium of a water board. Faced with a refuse disposal problem, Government financial pressure again compelled the taking into partnership of adjoining Urban District Councils to plan a large facility which would serve the area as a whole. Ironically the scheme was aborted in 1974 when a metropolitan wide solution became possible under the Metropolitan County Council. Even more ironically, Stockport battled against a proposal to amalgamate its police force with that of Greater Manchester. By determined advocacy and lobbying it kept its police out of the metropolis. The force could not remain separate but was merged with the Cheshire Constabulary. Six years later that victory proved Pyrrhic as the police force was unscrambled out of Cheshire and transferred to the new Greater Manchester Police Authority.

The relationship of the community to the Council also changed. Organised resistance at public inquiries persuaded councils of the need for public relations. Almost for the first time major consultation exercises started to be mounted in response to public pressure. Persuasion began to replace compulsion. Policies like house improvement required active collaboration from the public, unlike their slum clearance predecessors. Advocacy became more important. Councils strove to persuade Regional Planning Councils that the latters' regional plans should recognise local aspirations.

All these developments increased appreciation of the need for networking skills in local government. The 1974 reorganisation brought these skills into sharp focus. Alarmed by the sundering of county and district, the 1972 Bains Committee recommended dialogue through joint committees of representatives of County and District Councils. The newly created policy units found ready employment in the production of papers for the meetings. The joint committees were conspicuously unsuccessful. In principle they were to address the strategic level of policy making. At best they became talking shops. At worst they became vehicles for mutual sabotage. Understandably district representatives were unwilling to surrender either historic or newly won powers in deference to the County's strategic role or structure plan.

In West Yorkshire the County–District Joint Committee agreed in June 1974 that the Metropolitan County Council had a possible role in the field of recreation and the arts in, for example, the development of regional facilities. By the time the County Council had produced a consultative policy document on County Council initiatives the Districts had determined that recreation and arts should be entirely a district function. Outright condemnation by the districts followed and the County eventually retreated by abolishing the Recreation and Arts Department as an independent unit. The united view of the districts triumphed despite the clear intention of the County Council to discriminate in favour of less well provided districts.

The collapse of the County–District Joint Committees outlined the difficulties of trading across functional boundaries. Vested interests and professional rivalries often played a larger part than political differences.

The problems of cross-power negotiations were epitomised in Birmingham, where, following a dispute, the West Midlands County Council ended the agency agreement with Birmingham City Council whereby the latter undertook winter gritting. The County Council took over and cleared the snow. So did the City Council. Double snow clearance continued for three years and the dispute ended in the High Court.

Frustrated, the County Councils turned to regional planning. The demise of the Economic Planning Councils had opened the way to non-statutory joint strategies. These were much easier to achieve: a clear geographical separation of powers made trading easier. Uncomfortable issues were fudged in the interests of producing a plausible document which would argue for a greater regional share of the national cake. As general advocacy, the documents had limited influence on Governmental expenditure programmes. At a more specific level successes were recorded.

The Yorkshire and Humberside Strategic Conference of County Councils embraced enthusiastically a scheme whereby the colliery spoil of West and South Yorkshire could be transported to Humberside and used to reclaim mud flats in the Humber Estuary. The scheme was in the interests of the three County Councils and had no effect upon the fourth member, North Yorkshire. European money was sought and received for a feasibility study and a European Conference stage-managed in Leeds to broadcast the possibilities.

Collaboration between the statutory agencies on project management was distinctly more successful than collaboration on strategy. Such collaboration arose at an operational level. It was solidified by the statutory processes for control of expenditure priorities: Housing Investment Programme, the Transportation Plans and Programme and the Water Authority Annual Plan. Formal inter-organisational groups were buttressed by the use of personal networks and professional bonds. Engineers professionally agreed that development was an end good in itself; with that agreement on the ultimate goal they were able to find projects which attracted their professional support.

Protagonists from different professions found it much more difficult to agree
on mechanisms: they did not share a common overall objective.

The bonds of professionalism had also become irksome to local authorities. They no longer fitted the main preoccupations of members. The
problems of the inner cities, the campaign for the Welsh language, aggressive
equal opportunities policies transcended professionally-based departments.
Crucially local authorities began to see unemployment and loss of prosperity
as a main pre-occupation. The traditional local authority role of land preparation and servicing was extended to provision of sites and buildings. Derelict
mills were converted to flatted factories. Promotional publicity was stepped
up. Neither proved sufficient to counteract declining employment as footloose
employers disappeared from the scene.

The new solutions, member-inspired, crossed professional boundaries.
Direct action to create employment was taken. Contract compliance clauses
required the use of local labour. Authorities provided and ran serviced
accommodation for small businesses. More direct and innovative action was
taken by the creation of enterprise companies, owned or controlled by the
local authority. These companies, freed from the restraints of statutory
powers, municipal bureaucracy and public accountability, were able to prop
up declining firms and pump finance through loans or equity sharing into
new or expanding companies. Gaps in local enterprise provision were stopped:
export promotions, research and development were put at the service of small
firms. Enterprise agencies were formed to help create new businesses in
conjunction with Chambers of Commerce. Science parks were created in
partnership with universities. Equity finance was secured from the private
sector or even municipal pension funds.

Spectacular successes were matched by equally spectacular disasters. But
local authorities had learned an important lesson. They were no longer
prisoners of the statutory services they provided. They could take a view of
the economy of their areas. What was more, their resources gave them a lever
on other agencies through which they could make a direct impact.

The corporate local authority has been transcended and become an inter-
corporate agency.

## The future of local government

The ninth decade of the twentieth century saw sustained central government
concern about local government. Throughout the decade a war was waged to
contain local government spending and impose a regime of financial strin-
gency. The Rate Support Grant mechanisms have been used as much to
contain local government spending as to distribute grant. The ultimate
sanction of rate capping has been introduced.

Partly out of distrust and dissatisfaction with local government and partly
out of the desire to roll back the frontiers of the State, local government
powers have been eroded. The Training Agency (formerly the Manpower
Services Commission and the Training Commission) has taken over a major
part of the local education authorities' post-school role – to the tune now of
£2 billion of direct Government funding. The Royal Commission recommendations on a local authority based Prosecution Service were discounted

in favour of a national service. Airports have been severed from direct local authority control by the formation of limited companies at Government insistence. Central Government task forces have been installed in the inner cities. Two pilot Urban Development Corporations were established in London and Liverpool Docklands. Specific grants started to be debated – and introduced in the education field. Public transport was deregulated to break local monopolies. The strategic planning role of the Counties has been eroded to disappearing point. The abolition of the GLC and the Metropolitan Counties transferred powers exercised by Local Authorities to joint boards. The new Use Classes Order weakened the power of local authorities over development control. The use by local authorities of publicity was restricted.

The 1987/8 legislative programme contained a number of measures which will fundamentally affect the way local authorities operate for the rest of the century and beyond. Council tenants will be able to choose their landlords and break away from local authority control. Housing Action Trusts will take over inner city problem estates. Polytechnics have been removed from local authority direction. Independent City Technology Colleges have been introduced. Local authority schools can opt out of Council control and become grant maintained directly by the Department of Education and Science. More Urban Development Corporations have been created. The changes represent a major cultural shift from the 1960s commitment to involving the people through participation in the political process. The new theme is to regard people as customers, who can show their satisfaction or otherwise with services through freedom of choice and the right to shop around.

In some cases the nature of services provided directly by the local authority will change through a change in the nature of the relationship between the Council and the administration providing the service. Local authority services will be subject to tendering out and even if retained in-house will prompt an arm's-length relationship with the Direct Labour Organisation. Governing bodies and headteachers will be given independent status in the way in which schools are run, in regard to the curriculum, staffing and financial management. The Treasurer, charged with collection of the community charge, is given independent statutory powers in respect of which he can have recourse to the Secretary of State. The Government's response to the Widdicombe Report canvasses further independent statutory duties for the Treasurer. In these areas of his activity his role nears that of the Chief Constable, with an independent statutory responsibility. Local authority companies are to be confined within the statutory powers and finances of the local authority. The loss of control of the local non-domestic rate will affect the relationship between the local authority and its commercial ratepayers – and make the Council more dependent upon Central Government funds, which will now approach three-quarters of local government spending.

This process is not without its ironies. At a time of decline in powers local authorities have attracted more political importance than ever before. As freedom of parental choice in education is emphasised, the national curriculum will restrict it – at least in the state schools. As accountability is increased through the community charge local authorities face a diminution in powers. As the local Councils become less important in their powers they become more politicised.

The introduction of the community charge may well emphasise the trend towards local pluralism, with power scattered among a variety of agencies. Greeted with unpalatable rises in the community charge, precedent suggests that central government will look at the removal of further powers from local authorities so that they can be centrally financed. Education, as the biggest spending service and one where the local authorities' role becomes largely supportive, is widely canvassed as a candidate. The attachment of the police service to local government is threatened. The urgent need to review the relationship between the health service and social services makes community care a candidate for national transfer. Housing will disappear from local authority control progressively.

The mission of the Government is to move the local authority from being a direct provider of services to stimulating, facilitating, enabling and monitoring. It is to become the 'enabling authority'. It is possible to exaggerate this movement. There is no doubt, even when the effects of the legislative programme have worked through, that local authorities will continue to be major providers of services. Nevertheless the trend towards the use of other agencies and indirect provision prompts thoughts of a further structural reorganisation of local government.

British local authorities are among the largest in the Western world. Their size was caused by a view of the cost-effective minimum size to provide comprehensive services. If those services are not provided directly by the local authority the compulsion towards size disappears. The lesson of the abolition of the Metropolitan Counties and the GLC has been interpreted as a signal for the removal of the Shire Counties. If the conurbations can manage without a strategic body, then why should not the Shire Counties? More fundamentally, if services are to be acquired from discrete agencies by local authorities – or simply facilitated or regulated – councils could be reidentified with local communities. The monsters of 1974 could disintegrate.

Already a multiplicity of agencies, with differing boundaries and objectives, tackle local administration. Some of these agencies can be seen as competitors to the local authority – and the Audit Commission has urged local authorities to view them in that light. Consumer services and cost efficiency will be improved if competition is introduced. In so far as that concept increases cost effectiveness and improves consumer services then it must be welcomed. If, however, the consequence (as would be the case in the private sector) is that the agencies keep competitors at arm's length, then it is unlikely to be successful in improving services to consumers.

Collaborative pressures are great. Strategies pursued by one agency can well have cost implications for another. Consumers have an extremely inaccurate knowledge of who actually provides services. The public service ethic, still widespread, prompts protagonists to see the public sector as serving the public as a whole in a joint exercise. Every catastrophe summons forth a cry for greater collaboration.

In the 1960s solutions to local authorities' problems appeared within grasp: continued increased resources and a little time would solve them. Now the true complexity of problems is better understood. The Griffiths Report on Community Care (1988), following a succession of similar reports, drew the obvious conclusion that health and social services must work collaboratively in tackling the problems caused by the mentally handicapped and increasing numbers of elderly. The increasing number of homeless families calls for liaison between Housing Departments and Social Services Departments – as well as other agencies. Urban regeneration can only be attacked through multi-disciplinary effort. Crime prevention can no longer be seen as something which the police can deal with alone: a problem for society as a whole, the Home Office continually underlines the need for all agencies – especially local authorities – to collaborate energetically. The Department of Trade and Industry urges the participation of local authorities in their initiatives to help employment. The Butler–Sloss Inquiry into the Cleveland Child Abuse Cases (1988) showed the need for joint working between police, social services and the health service. The London Docklands Development Corporation, after seven years of going it alone, now pursues energetically collaboration with its local authority neighbours, without whom its social role cannot be fulfilled. An information based society will prompt agencies to joint effort.

Thus paradoxically the incipient change in provision of local services may be seen as increasing the need for formal collaborative mechanisms. Whereas a local authority may fudge strategic issues and deal with problems ad hoc, two or more distinct agencies sharing a problem need a system of joint working. Separate agencies will be under increasing pressure to rely not only on personal and informal networks – often very effective on single issues – but to create properly understood and formally recognised mechanisms. In the 1960s public servants worried about creating a consistent corporate interface for the local authority to present to its consumers. That pressure remains and will continue to prompt efforts to overcome the difficulties caused by a public sector where services are fragmented across organisational boundaries.

Within this dichotomy lies the kernel of optimism for the future of local government – the enabling authority.

# 2 Bringing order to chaos: the role of the enabling authority

**Key points**

▲ *As direct service provision contracts, so the local authority will seek a wider role of influence over its area though exercised through other agencies. It will seek to establish networks with agencies which are key to its plans*
▲ *Local networks already exist in every area and are vital to its running*
▲ *The local authority often plays a key role in these networks*
▲ *When looking at a total concept of service provision or problem solving, the local authority will usually have to rely on external agencies. The nature of its relationships with these bodies will determine the extent to which the authority can exercise influence*
▲ *External agencies are key to the provision of choice to the residents of the area*
▲ *Planning is essential – but should be restricted to key issues*
▲ *Anticipate crises: it is much easier to head off a crisis than to solve it when it has developed*
▲ *Look for convergent strategies, both within the local authority and outside*
▲ *Internal management structures, preoccupations and skills will change profoundly so as to reflect a wider role for the Council*

## The concept of enabling

While local authorities have never regarded themselves as tied to their statutory powers, their interventions in other areas have been relatively sporadic and unplanned until the recent past. As direct service provision diminishes, so is member time freed to devote to more general concerns. The powers allocated to local government in Britain follow no international or accepted norm; their allocation is fairly arbitrary. So councillors will see no reason to confine themselves to an arbitrary and contracting arena. They – or their visionary successors – will have as a main concern the overall welfare of their area. They will seek practical ways of influencing other agencies to achieve a desirable result. Enabling, in other words ensuring local choice, will be the main theme. As a concept this covers a range from job creation to services to the handicapped. There is no choice without an available job; no choice if access is impossible.

But the enabling council will not be the only or even the main provider of this pluralistic choice. The change will require a different structure, different priorities and different skills both for members and for officers. The managerial consequences on the local authority will be profound. Key to its success will be the way in which it can establish relationships with the external agencies which provide services, the way in which it can establish networks with other bodies.

## The nature of relationships

The extent to which a local authority can influence an external agency depends on the relationship between the two bodies. A contractor or voluntary body depending on council support will behave in a way very different from an independent private company or tier of government. The nature of the relationship seems so fundamental to management beyond the organisational boundaries of the local authority that the remaining chapters of the book are structured around the different kinds of relationship. Methods and resources deployed do overlap, but I have minimised duplication.

Relationships between the local authority and external agencies fall into these categories:

▽ *Control* Where the local authority controls a third party such as a contractor.
▽ *Partial control* Where the local authority controls some parts of the operation of an agency but not others, e.g. police, schools.
▽ *Partnership* Where the local authority and the external agency agree to collaborate in a common aim.
▽ *Part ownership* Where the local authority is a constituent member of a composite body.
▽ *Purchasing* Where the local authority can use its purchasing power to affect suppliers and manufacturers.
▽ *Support* Where the local authority supports an external agency, usually a voluntary body, in its activities.
▽ *Regulatory* Where the local authority has licensing or enforcement powers enabling it to regulate some part of the agency's activities.
▽ *The capacity to influence* Where there is no obvious nexus between the local authority and the agency which the local authority wishes to influence.

## Local networks

In every area there is a network of relationships between the local authority and the public, private and voluntary sector agencies which operate in the area. The local authority's traffic engineers and licensing officers work with the police. Social Services Departments collaborate with the Health Service. The local authority nominates members to outside organisations and to joint committees. The Council and the Chamber of Commerce interact on the level of the rates – and usually on areas of mutual benefit to the economy. Developers relate to the Council. The local authority seeks to persuade its people to improve their houses, stop their dogs fouling the footpath and not to drop litter in the streets.

Most of these relationships are operational, forged by officers who need collaboration to achieve their goal. Some are strategic, like joint campaigns between Council and police to control the sex industry or between Council and British Coal to reclaim derelict land. Some, like campaigns aimed at the public, are designed to influence actors on the local scene.

Many relationships operate without the intervention of the local authority. Many more include the local authority as a key actor. The networks form sinews without which the area cannot operate. They are for the most part, taken for granted and assume prominence only in times of crisis. Sometimes a difficult personal relationship can bring a relationship into prominence. At other times a divergence of aim between organisations secures public attention.

The local authority is not a neutral protagonist in these relationships. It (or its officers) usually wishes to influence or direct the other party. Other parties wish to influence or direct the local authority. Even when there is a convergence of view there will often be a difference of priority. The networks may be sterile or fruitful, but they will exist none the less. They may include or exclude councillors. Through them the enabling authority will influence the welfare of its area often in fields beyond the confines of its statutory services – and in its turn be influenced.

## Why local authorities have to be involved

No local authority in the country confines itself to its statutory functions. Few can, for example, resist the pressure to oppose the closure of a local hospital. Indeed the local council is a statutory consultee on many matters outside its strict remit. Even the exercise of its statutory powers often implies collaboration, formal or informal and the authority will wish to influence actions in ways which will be beneficial to its residents. A variety of motives lie behind the compulsion on local authorities to sway others:

1   A Council's statutory powers compel it to interact with outside agencies. In the exercise of those powers the authority will have developed policies which it will seek to impose on the other party. Thus an applicant for planning permission will be required to comply with the authority's overall plan. The authority will often try to go beyond its statutory powers by securing benefits, wherever it can, for its residents. In imposing conditions for a planning application or a licence it will have regard to the welfare of its people.

2   Few Councils would disclaim in total a responsibility for the general welfare of their area. In the words of the Federal Trust for Education and Research: 'Whether services are provided publicly or privately, and whether there is devolution to consumers or to individual schools or to housing trusts, priorities for the local community have still to be determined' (Bogdanor *et al.* 1988.) Thus in 1988 the City of Westminster campaigned vigorously against the proposed closure of the Westminster Hospital. In 1986 the St Helens Council joined the management and workforce of the Pilkington Glass Manufacturers to fight off a takeover

bid from an international conglomorate. When in 1988, Nestlé and Suchard made rival bids for Rowntree, the Lord Mayor of York set off for Switzerland to fight the proposed takeover.

3   The Council may have an ideological goal which it seeks to impose on its area. Thus the Gwynedd County Council sees the preservation and propagation of the Welsh language as a policy which both underpins and transcends all its activities. The City of Westminster has a vigorous policy to staunch the loss of residential population in its City, a policy against which it judges not only its own activities but those of all other agencies – including the private sector – in the City.

4   In a crisis the buck tends to stop with the local Council, whose politicians are usually saddled with responsibility for explaining it. In the Cleveland child abuse case, the lack of communication between the Health Authority, Police and Local Authority was at the root of the 1987 crisis. As the most public and accessible of the actors, Cleveland County Council gained much of the unwelcome limelight.

5   Where there is a co-ordination vacuum, the local authority is propelled into the role by default. The Home Office, for example, created Juvenile Crime Panels including Police, Housing, Social Services, Probation, Education, The Youth Service, MSC, Adult Education, Further Education and voluntary bodies. Little came of the initiative until local authorities were charged with co-ordinating it. The Royal Society for the Prevention of Accidents presses local authorities to make the public aware of the dangers of accidents in the home and, indeed, seeks to make home accident prevention a mandatory responsibility of local authorities. There is no other body which could take on this role.
The local authority may voluntarily fill a vacuum lest an opportunity be lost or channelled into undesirable results. Thus Kent County Council, faced with the Channel Tunnel, set up in 1988 a unit to conceptualise its impact upon the County and to co-ordinate a response among all local agencies so as to minimise problems and maximise opportunities.

6   Local politicians need the support of the electorate. They are naturally anxious to secure favourable publicity. Indeed favourable publicity to a politician is as catnip to cats. They will not wish to miss an opportunity to be seen to respond to public wishes. In some cases this may result in the creation of a campaign of sustained pressure. In others an ad hoc response to a particular issue may be almost thrust upon Councillors by sustained public interest. Thus the West Yorkshire Metropolitan County Council and its Leader, John Gunnell, became major actors in the sad case of Helen Smith, the West Yorkshire nurse who died in Saudi Arabia under mysterious circumstances – despite the tenuous link with the County Council's functions as custodian of the mortuary and funder of the Coroner's service.

7   Councils may well retain a close interest in services once theirs but now elsewhere. In part this may result from personal interests; in part from

reluctance to see the new organisation's objectives replace their former plans; and in part a general concern for their area's welfare. Thus the Docklands local authorities maintain pressure on the London Docklands Development Corporation to secure a greater proportion of spending on community services. Local authority health committees take a wide view of community services. In some cases this pressure may relate to services which the local authority never operated but would like to – hence the proliferation of Police Committees among inner London boroughs.

8    As local authorities become closer to their customers, they become aware that there are multi-dimensional needs that their own services cannot meet in full. They may see it as part of their remit to persuade other agencies to improve service delivery to their residents. Hence the large number of welfare rights take-up campaigns, which in some cases are said to have had spectacular success. Strathclyde claim an extra £4 million of benefits were procured following a campaign in their area.

9    The local authority is increasingly seen as a consumer watchdog. In 1988 Sir Philip Woodfield's scrutiny report on the 'Supervision of Charities' proposed that all local charities should be required to send a copy of their accounts to the relevant local authority. Some Councils may resent an imposed burden of this kind; others may already have taken the initiative by reorganising charities in their area so as to maximise benefits from hitherto dormant organisations. There is a consensus that Councils should encourage choice for their residents. To quote Secretary of State, Nicholas Ridley:

> If a variety of providers is desirable then the Council needs to work out how to encourage diversity and fruitful competition. If regulation is needed then the task is to find out how to do this fairly, efficiently and swiftly without stifling initiative and enterprise (Ridley, N. 1988).

These examples illustrate the range of pressures which will prompt the local authority more and more to intervene in the field of pluralistic provision. There will, of course, be wide divergences between the extent to which this will happen. To some extent political differences between Councils will prompt different responses; more relevant will often be historic attitudes. Most relevant of all will be the degree of public pressure which surrounds any issue. If the extent of response differs, there is a general commitment to a view wider than the Council's functions.

## The role of the local authority

To quote Nicholas Ridley: 'Authorities will need to operate in a more pluralist way than in the past, alongside a wide variety of public, private and voluntary agencies. It will be their task to stimulate and assist these other agencies to play their part instead of, or as well as, making provision themselves' (Ridley, N., 1988).

As the conduit for pluralism, the enabling authority will maximise the range of choices available to its residents – supplementing the private sector in areas where that sector does not provide a choice. A precondition of action

is information. The consumers themselves must have information if they are
to exercise a choice. In its development plan for education (1988) the City of
Westminster proposes to use terminals in its public libraries to enable its
residents to obtain comparative data on the performance of schools. Area
information systems, comparing local services, may well become more widely
available using libraries as public information points. The local authority will
itself need geographic information systems if it is to be aware of deficiencies
in choice. Only when it receives that information can it take action to stimulate
provision. Thus the City of Bradford in *The Changing Face of Bradford* (1984)
produced a series of profiles which looked at the problems of the City ward
by ward, showing clearly deficiencies in existing provision. With the benefit
of such information remedial action can be taken to improve the local
authority's own services. It can also prompt other agencies to improve or
restructure their own service delivery.

## How to plan without being swamped by paper

There is one grave danger in macro-planning of this nature. That is that an
unnecessary quest for completeness will swamp the relevant information –
hence the collapse of the planning, programming and budgeting systems of
the 1970s. The classic example is the Greater London Development Plan,
four years in preparation, three in consideration and three in approval – a
plan which had ceased to fulfil its purpose when it was finally approved.

Discredited comprehensive planning has been largely replaced by the
notion of consumer sovereignty. Nevertheless action in a pluralistic society
still requires a strategy. There is a simple answer: identify the key issues and
plan for those. Put your eggs in many baskets is a concept replaced by that
of putting favourite eggs in one basket and watching that basket very closely.

Issue-based planning will usually start by contemplation of the action a
local authority can take through direct service provision. It will be rare,
though, for a major problem to be tackled successfully within the confines of
the Council's statutory powers. The commitment to take effective action will
prompt the local authority to look outside the confines of its own services.

When General Motors announced the virtual closure of their truck plant
in South Bedfordshire in 1986 over 3000 redundancies swelled an already
high unemployment rate. The action prompted the three local authorities
concerned to joint action. The strategy produced innovative approaches
within the authorities' own services: targetting personnel policies to
provide jobs for the unemployed; using their purchasing policies to
support the local economy; providing factory units for firms to expand
or relocate; a land use strategy to concentrate business expansion in the
most appropriate areas. The strategy went further: image promotion;
a concentration on retraining; support to an enterprise agency and a
development agency. In recognising that the three local authorities had
to give clear leadership in the development and implementation of the
economic strategy, it was recognised that they had to do so in close
partnership and in coalition with other bodies – local industrialists, trade
unions and community organisations. The strategy identified the major
employers and prompted a closer consultative relationship to give earlier

warning of investment and employment plans; a campaign for increased General Motors investment in the UK; the possibility of making available venture capital through an enterprise board; and the setting-up of an economic development council to provide a forum for public, private, voluntary and community sector bodies to formulate a long term economic development strategy. The closure prompted an even wider horizon: contributions to European policy planning on disclosure of information and the social responsibilities of big firms to their communities; joint lobbying for increased investment in the third world to restore demand for commercial vehicles; and for the removal of the special car tax.

Just as preservation or creation of employment can prompt a multi-organisational strategy, so can unemployment itself:

North Tyneside Metropolitan Borough Council, faced with long term unemployment, formulated a strategy to improve services to unemployed people. The Council created a recruitment scheme for unemployed people on its own staff; introduced launchpad grants to long term unemployed to enable them to develop hobbies or pursue self-motivated initiatives; subsidised day trips for unemployed. The strand ran through many of the services provided by the Council. Outside the Council's own activities, financial support was provided for the development of unemployed centres run by the voluntary sector; peripatetic development workers were appointed to support the voluntary sector; outdoor activities for unemployed people were developed. The voluntary sector participated in developing the response with equal status to officers of the local authority.

Other problems prompt multi-organisational strategies:

Westminster City Council, alarmed by an outflow of residents which reduced its population from 250 000 to 175 000 in two decades, formed a policy to build stable communities. Its key element was the provision of middle income housing. Extensive programmes of re-use of the Council's own housing stock were devised: stepping-up a right to buy campaign; designating whole blocks of flats for sale; provision of grants to those prepared to relinquish their tenancy of Council dwellings. Home-steading was encouraged as was provision for starter flats on suitable sites. Land disposal policies insisted on provision of middle income housing. Planning policies were used to press for the inclusion of resi-dential units in all suitable developments. Pressure was mounted to restore offices with temporary planning consents to residential use. Enforcement was stepped-up on the misuse of flats as holiday or short term lets. Residents' parking permits were limited to residents spending four nights each week in the City. Attention was given to those aspects of the environment which could encourage permanent residential uses: increase in residents' car parking spaces and preferential terms for resi-dents' parking in Council owned car parks. The advantages of residence were promoted through a residents' card, conferring concessionary rates on residents not only in Council facilities but in many private facilities in the City. Arts organisations, for example, seeking grants from the City Council, were encouraged to make concessions to the Council's residents.

The preservation of good health and education facilities was identified as a key factor which could encourage residents to stay in the City.

It is often too late to take effective action when a crisis has arisen. Occasionally a St Helens may be successful in helping to fight off a predator. More often, as in York and Rowntrees, the situation will be beyond rescue when it comes to public attention. Plans by a District Health Authority for closure of a hospital are not immutable. But they are very much easier to prevent in the first place: if the presence of a hospital is seen as vital to the life of a town action should be taken before formal closure is bruited.

In 1988 Pilkingtons contemplated a major expansion in Kent, to take advantage of the Channel Tunnel: a major decision for a company historically concentrated in St Helens. The decision had great significance for the town: loss of extra jobs; the prospective run-down of existing production capacity and employment; and a potential dilution of the historic commitment of the company to the community. Because of the closeness of company and local authority (cemented by the alliance over the previous failed take-over) the Council were well aware of the possibility. They were able to arouse public concern, orchestrate a substantial press campaign and generally raise the level of awareness so as to put considerable pressure on the company. Had such plans been hatched in secret by the company, unknown to the Council – and a decision to build elsewhere taken – it would have been immeasurably more difficult to affect the issue.

Anticipation is vital. This implies a knowledge of the key areas of concern; the development of personal relationships with those involved in the key agencies; and the devotion of resources – notably time – to the problem. The arrival of Marshall Bluecher at Waterloo was very welcome but would have been even more so had he arrived twenty-four hours earlier.

Some problems cannot be anticipated, but the institutions responsible are obvious. If a factory, university or hospital is seen as vital to the welfare of the community, then close liaison must be maintained even if no difficulties are on the horizon. This will ensure that the local authority becomes quickly aware of looming disasters and is in a better position to take avoiding action. Other issues are self-identifying: it is crucial for the local authority to take a total view of their impact on the area and co-ordinate the agencies affected.

The Channel Tunnel is due to open in May 1993. The Kent County Council has developed a holistic strategy with a thirty year time frame. A Channel Tunnel Co-ordinator has been appointed to the Chief Executive's office. His role is to ensure a strategic approach – providing early warnings of possible problems and a rapid response to changing circumstances. The County Council had joined with its opposite number across the Channel – the Nord/Pas de Calais Region – to promote their areas jointly to industry in the US, Japan and Germany. Training, especially in French and German, is a priority. Infrastructure investment is planned for the East Kent area around the international passenger station at Ashford – an area which has not shared in the general South-East boom. Careful planning surrounds partnerships with the private sector, with an aim of attracting industries connected with new technology, business services and, obviously, distribution. Liaison is maintained with District Councils in order to influence their planning decisions. Long-term effects, like international commuting, are being assessed in terms of their impact on the county.

## Convergent and divergent strategies

An attractive method of corporate planning is to trace through the policy objectives of the Council and see whether their strategies converge. Convergent strategies are relatively easy to implement: organisational resistance is minimised. On the other hand major policy objectives often result in divergent strategies. If progress is to be made these strategies have to be reconciled. The same constraints apply even more markedly in inter-agency collaboration. If the organisations have convergent strategies then ready collaboration is achieved. This may not need to reach beyond the operational level.

Often public sector agencies have divergent strategies. Their objectives are, by definition, different. A method has to be found of reconciling the two.

The Bloomsbury Health Authority, faced with the perennial cash crisis of the National Health Service, proposed to rationalise its properties in the City of Westminster. This policy diverged from the City Council's policy of maintaining the present standards of health care. On the other hand the City Council had a divergent policy of securing more homes in order to maintain residential accommodation in the City. By negotiation and by using the planning process, the City Council sought a balance of adequate health care – while at the same time increasing the number of residential units. The divergent substantive policies of the two authorities could be reconciled by invocation of a third but convergent policy.

Once a local authority has a view of the provision it wishes to see in its area – or the choices to be made available to its residents – it can identify the organisations which are key to its plans, whether public or private. It can also identify the organisations with which it is most frequently in contact.

## How to watch the external environment

Councils, like most organisations, tend to be introspective. If Councils are to assume a new role as enablers, regulators, monitors, creators of choice, they must be turned outwards, taking a synoptic view of their area. Councillors are, of course, key to this process. Not only do their attitudes shape those of the local authority, but they are a major source of interaction between the community and the Council. Their own contacts with constituents, ward political parties and voluntary organisations make them aware of many key concerns of the locality. However part-time councillors rarely have the time or personal resources to approach such issues systematically, to anticipate problems or to sustain a regular dialogue with agencies external to the local authority. Officer time must be set aside to encompass such relationships. The objectives or key tasks set for Chief Officers can define key relationships and require attention to be given to them.

Arun District Council has examined its residents' needs and identified as key issues the ageing population and unemployment. To respond to these issues the professional management structure of the authority has been abandoned and replaced by four departments:

Housing and Community Care – responsible for personal services;
Environment and Leisure – responsible for public services;
Planning and Economic Development – responsible for district services;
Finance and Administration.

The new organisation is intended to free managers from the constraints of professional boundaries and to take a holistic approach to the problems of the area.

Once a Council has identified organisations key to its plans, the Council can identify also the key actors in those organisations, earmark allies and collaborators and create a relationship. Convergent strategies may prompt a strategic relationship and a formal implementation structure. Divergent strategies must be reconciled or, if this is not possible, a sustained campaign must be mounted.

Key to reconciliation will be the nature of the relationships between the local authority and the other agency. If the outside organisation is in any way dependent upon the local authority, e.g. for funds or for a statutory permission, the chances of reconciling divergent strategies are very high. If, on the other hand, the local authority is the suppliant, then it may well be the local authority which has to jettison various sub-objectives in order to attain a higher goal. In either event a machinery for dialogue must be created.

## Beyond the local authority

As local authorities operate in a more pluralistic way, and are increasingly liberated from the provision of direct services, they will inevitably turn their minds to the services offered by the agencies which replace them. Freed from administrative detail, their members will have more time to consider the wider welfare of their areas. Officers no longer responsible for managing large departments will be able to take a strategic view of the entirety of provision in the area. The 1987 Housing White Paper says Councils 'should increasingly see themselves as enablers to ensure that everyone in their area is adequately housed; but not necessarily by them'. This concept has a much wider attraction. In the words of Professors George Jones and John Stewart: 'Councils should recognise that an effective role does not always require direct provision of a service. The role of a Council is widened if it is not limited to direct provision. It can then be the local government, acting as the community governing itself, concerned with all the problems and issues in the area, whichever agency, organisation or group is actually charged with the function or service, whether public or private, collective or voluntary'.

## The French example

Such a view of local government is taken by French communes. Relatively powerless by British standards, they are yet enormously influential. Having few direct responsibilities they are able to concentrate their resources on the overall welfare of their areas. The prominence of the French Mayor is of vital importance: it is he who is the spokesman for the area. On him rests the burden of procuring the desired results from other providers. In this he is greatly helped by the French *cumul des mandats* system. The Mayor may have a regional or national mandate as well as his local responsibilities. He may indeed be Prime Minister. No French politician would abandon his local power base in the way which is axiomatic in Britain. No local commune would expect it. They would want their Mayor to use his new-found influence to benefit their locality. Seemingly powerless local councils may, in fact, be a force in the land, not capable of being overlooked.

## The Bradford view

*The Changing Face of Bradford*, the City of Bradford report, makes the same point in a British context:

> Faced with these trends the Council could decide to manage only those services that still remain under democratic local control. Alternatively it could seek also to influence and involve other organisations to ensure their policies are co-ordinated in the interest of Bradford as a whole.
>
> This would need a major effort by Councillors and officers to understand how those agencies work and to develop better links with them.
>
> The Council still may be able to make effective decisions in a climate of dwindling resources, but it will need genuinely to share power and responsibility.

## Managerial consequences for local authorities

The consequences of this change will ultimately have the most substantial effect upon local government. As local authorities become increasingly unencumbered by direct managerial responsibility then paradoxically the overall concept of their accountabilities will grow. If they are enablers, then they can enable in areas beyond their statutory responsibilities. The need for committees created to oversee the provision of a service, whether allotments, fire or education, will disappear. In their place will arise strategic committees with a vision of the entirety of provision in an area, whether provided by the local authority or not. Already this synoptic view has promoted the creation of committees not tied to service departments – on equal opportunities, women, economic development or health. Committees will be created to look sectorally at client groups like the elderly. Who are the gainers and losers in provision in the area? Members will seek a forum to express their concerns about their own constituencies. What issues should the Council take up? Councils will seek genuine measures of performance – the effect of their planning decisions on social and environmental structures, the impact of their transport policies. Complaints and marketing research will be used as barometers of public concern.

The Audit Commission (1989) sees the role of the local authority principally as policy maker and employer of contractors. As client, the Council should, the Commission says:

▽ assess consumer demand and satisfaction;
▽ develop new ideas on service provision and quality;
▽ define desired levels and quality of provision.

The enabling Council may see a similar role in relation to services for which it is not directly the client. Its watchdog role – emphasised by its existing regulatory powers – will become more important to its overall strategy. Dissemination of information to residents will be equally important. The roles of officers will divide. Managerial skills are required in those who will head the organisations providing services – whether internally or externally. Similar skills will be needed in central support units, which will survive only if they are competitive. Increasingly they will be financed through direct time-charging, often through service level agreements. Direct service organisations will look elsewhere for support if central units do not provide a cost-effective service.

The cadre of officers who serve the policy-making process will be recruited more for their strategic and political abilities than for their ability to run a vast professional bureaucracy. These officers will have a major pre-occupation with inter-organisational relationships and the creation of networks to achieve the Council's strategic goals. Their commitment and that of their Council will be to the overall welfare of their area, which will become of paramount importance. Hence this book.

## Conclusion

As facilitators, enablers and watchdogs, Councils will take an increasing interest in attacking the problems of their areas. They will be increasingly systematic in planning for key areas of concern. Committee structures will change to reflect overall Council goals. Officer structures will reflect the client-contractor split.

The Chief Executive and Chief Officers will see an increasingly role in looking outwards at their area as direct service provision by the local authority declines. Skills and preoccupations will change and be recognised in the objectives set them by the Council.

The importance of external agencies in service provision and the extension of consumer choice will be increasingly recognised by local authorities. Members and Chief Officers will spend more time in developing convergent strategies with external agencies and in developing joint networks for service provision. The provision of information to residents will become an important role for the enabling authority. The overall welfare of the area will become the local authority's paramount concern.

### Using this chapter

▲ *What concern does your Council have in issues which are beyond the direct control of the Council?*
▲ *Has your Authority carried out any systematic analysis of service provision or problems in its area?*
▲ *Does your Authority have a strategy for key issues affecting the area?*
▲ *Have other agencies been involved in the joint solution of their problems? Do*

*their policies lead to the joint solutions the Council seeks? If so are efforts synchronised through a joint network? If not are attempts made to reconcile policies and priorities through the identification of convergent policies?*

▲  *Does your Council study the plans of other agencies and seek to influence them?*
▲  *What time is set aside for dialogue and joint planning with external agencies?*
▲  *Does your Council merely react to crisis? Or does it seek to influence at an early stage the activities of outside agencies?*
▲  *Does your Council make available to residents information about the choices available to them?*
▲  *Does your Council's committee and management structure concentrate members' and managers' minds on problems internal to the local authority? Or does it focus on key issues to the locality, straddling organisational boundaries?*

# 3 Control: contracting out

## Key points

▲ *Specifications for contracted out services should include qualitative as well as quantitative measures*

▲ *The local authority must ensure its contract does not operate so as to shut out future competition*

▲ *Alternative arrangements must be possible if a contractor fails to perform satisfactorily*

▲ *Contracts must cater for changes in circumstances or variations during the contract period*

▲ *Contracting presents an opportunity to secure contributions towards enhanced specification*

## Experience of local authorities in using contractors

The ability of a local authority to influence an external agency depends on the relationship between the two. In theory the most straightforward relationship is between a local authority and a company which is contracted to deliver a service to it. The reality may be rather different. Local authorities have, of course, a long history of relationships with contractors. The overwhelming majority of local authority capital works has always been carried out by private contract and local authorities have developed a substantial expertise in controlling building and engineering contractors. The expertise extends into routine works of maintenance carried out on a schedule of rates. Highly effective service contracts have also been used by local authorities for many years.

> The West Yorkshire Metropolitan County Council inherited from the West Riding County Council the system of contracting with Pennine farmers for snow clearance and gritting of local roads. It was cheap for the County Council and employed farmers at a time when they would have no other occupation. It used existing plant – tractors and Land Rovers. It provided a speedy and effective attack on snow covered roads: a multiplicity of agents could operate simultaneously in a way which no centralised provision could offer cost effectively. Moreover it relied on a highly motivated work force: the farmers themselves were cut off until they had cleared the roads.

## The new requirements

Nevertheless most local authorities are still relatively inexperienced in contracting out entire services. They are now required to tender out services by statutory compulsion. The direct labour organisation legislation of 1980 dipped a toe in the water. The Local Government Act 1988 extends the requirement to tender out to other services. So far refuse collection, building cleaning, other cleaning, catering for schools and welfare, other catering, ground maintenance, vehicle maintenance and leisure centres have been identified by the Government. A timetable has been issued to which local authorities must work in preparing specifications and inviting tenders. Using a different process, refuse disposal is also scheduled for tendering out.

Some authorities have already contracted out some of these services. For the overwhelming majority it will be a new experience. They are not short of advice. Every consultant in the country is anxious to help and a variety of guidance notes have been prepared by the Local Government Training Board, the Society of Local Authority Chief Executives, the Association of Metropolitan Authorities and others. The guidance understandably concentrates on the process of drawing up specifications, contracts and tender lists.

Most of this book is about how the enabling council can take a positive managerial perspective in areas outside its direct control. Contractors are in theory under the client's direct control. Nevertheless there are clear limits on what a Council can achieve from a contractor. This chapter concentrates on the pitfalls which may prevent a local authority from obtaining from a contractor the service it requires – both in the short- and long-term. The relationship needs as much thought and strategic thinking as any other.

## The specification

The copious literature is less than specific on how the continuing relationship with a contractor will be managed. At the most basic level the contractor will not be susceptible to the same degree of day to day control by councillors as was the predecessor service organisation. Neither will be the successful direct labour organisation. The starting point of the relationship will be the specification of the contract. Local authorities are entirely free in drawing up the specification. Legislation is silent on what may be included or excluded. Authorities can specify outputs in terms of quantity and quality.

However both the contractor and the direct labour organisation will deliver no more than is specified – at least without additional payment. This has forced a clarification of the mind of local authorities in terms of the service they wish to deliver. Often standards have historically been determined by inputs: the ability of the number of people employed to succeed in executing tasks. Vagueness about overall outputs permitted tasks to be specified almost on a daily basis. This system, though loose, had the advantage of being extremely responsive to daily needs and special demands by Councillors. Parks staff could be diverted to beautify the route of the Royal procession without worry about the consequences of neglect elsewhere.

This will change under the new arrangements. A specification which requires the delivery of a service to so-called existing standards may well cause an increase in costs. This is because the existing standards are not in practice delivered. There may be an aspiration to sweep the streets once a week; but management may know that because of absences and other pressures the de facto standard is once a fortnight. But if once a week is specified in the contract then both contractor and direct labour organisation will have to deliver to that specification. This process will concentrate the minds of councillors on the extent of the service which they feel the Council can afford.

Local authority architects have always been chary of overkeen pricing by contractors. They know that the contractor wishes to make a profit and, if an unduly keen price is quoted, will seek to turn every delay or variation to pecuniary advantage. Similarly variation orders issued to service contractors will be expensive if the contract does not contemplate a basis upon which they can be charged. Local authorities will also have to consider wider social objectives: differential charging for leisure centres for the old or the unemployed is an example. Different cleaning specifications may be laid down for different parts of the Council's area. The process of specification will impose a new discipline on local authorities. Those who baulk at the political decisions at specification stage will take the political consequences later.

Certain principles emerge to which a local authority must have regard if it is to have a successful relationship during the term of the contract with its new independent agency.

## 1   QUALITATIVE OUTPUTS

The specification will, of course, give quantitative outputs: the number of grass cuts per season; the hours of opening of the leisure centre; the frequency of cleaning. It is equally important to address the issue of qualitative outputs. Some may be capable of definition. The expertise of trading standards officers, environmental health officers and public analysts may well be of great help to client departments in monitoring quality.

Other qualitative outputs may be specified in more general terms. The specification for one local authority's grounds maintenance contract, for example, requires a contractor to have regard to the interests of users of the parks during maintenance operations like grass cutting and watering. A succession of drenched voters could give an impetus to the imposition of penalties under the contract. Even more general conditions may be imposed: the conditions of contract for street cleaning and refuse collection for the City of Westminster provide:

> The contractors shall provide their services at all times in such a manner as shall promote and enhance the image and reputation of the authority and its district.

The penalty clause allows the Council to impose a financial penalty on the contractor for breach. The sum specified is one

> which the authority and the contractor agree is a fair and reasonable sum having regard to the utmost importance attached by the authority as the local authority for the heart of London to maintaining and enhancing its image and reputation and to the damage to such image and reputation likely to be caused by a failure or default on the part of the contractor (SOLACE/LGTB 1988).

General qualitative provisions may be difficult to define and more difficult to enforce; but they certainly cannot be enforced if they are not present in the contract. The consequences of an inadequate service will rebound upon the local authority. Its residents will not accept that blame attaches solely to the contractor. The local authority will be under pressure to remedy the deficiencies. It can only do so within the terms of the contract.

## 2  INSPECTION AND MONITORING

All advice stresses the importance of the inspection and monitoring function after the contract has been let. Both the private sector and local authority employees suffer from a common defect of humanity. Without vigilance standards will decline, corners will be cut and the opportunity taken either to make greater profits or to go home early, as the case may be. The London Borough of Wandsworth, a widely-acclaimed pioneer of privatisation, found it necessary to increase its inspectorate after contracting out if it was to maintain contracts at a satisfactory standard.

Some advice has proposed a centralised contract monitoring department. There are certainly virtues in a proposal which would concentrate expertise in one place. It would, though, be vital to ensure that such a department included professionals with specialist expertise in the areas contracted out. A general administrator, however otherwise effective, would not be able to maintain quality standards on, say, horticultural maintenance. The creation of a central contracts department may dilute expertise, with some professionals being left in the client department and others divorced from it. Whichever option is chosen it is important that the quality and expertise of the inspectorate is maintained. Moreover the residual in-house professionals must retain the responsibility for planning the future of the service – a new leisure centre, new waste disposal sites, etc.

## 3  PRESERVATION OF COMPETITION

All the contracts will come to an end. They may be renewed. But authorities must take care that they have not prejudiced their competitive position at the end of the contract by locking themselves irretrievably to one contractor. In some unusual cases this may be unavoidable. The City of Westminster, for example, lets the rights to a Christmas Funfair in Leicester Square. By a convention of the Showmen's Guild no showman will bid for a site after one showman has established a fair for three years. Such a case is, though, highly unusual. Specific steps can usually be taken to protect the authority's interest. For example it will be normal for an authority to retain ownership of a depot, giving a licence only to a contractor to occupy it. This would enable the depot to be relicensed to any new contractor at the expiry of the contract. If a new contractor had to provide a new depot it could effectively render any rival bids out of court. The same may well apply to vehicles and plant. Commonly local authorities would license their successful contractor to use their vehicles and plant but retain ownership. New vehicles and plant would be subject to repurchase by the local authority at an agreed valuation at the end of the contract – thus making them immediately available for any successor. Quite apart from the cost of new plant, the time spent on delivery could effectively rule out any rival bids unless such a clause were included. Similar considerations apply to other contracts.

In some cases there may be a limited number of private contractors who are prepared to tender. Research following deregulation in the bus industry suggests that the more operators which bid for a contract, the lower the cost will be. Local authorities can consider what approaches to tendering out will encourage the entry of new (usually small) contractors. In deciding which tender to accept, a local authority may be able to have regard to the long-term implications of securing the entry of a new contractor into the market.

## 4   ALTERNATIVES

Though no substitute for collaborative working, in order to ensure performance local authorities will commonly include in their contract conditions a regime of penalties, including the right to recover the cost of work done in default. The penalty clauses will, no doubt, be carefully drafted to ensure that they are within the law. The contracts will also provide for determination in the event of inadequate performance. In this case bonds or guarantees will take care of any financial loss suffered by the local authority.

A local authority can thus protect itself from pecuniary embarrassment; but this is no substitute for having available an alternative contractor who can step into the breach. Gross failure to perform may prompt a wish to terminate a contract quickly. This cannot be done unless an alternative is in the wings. If a direct labour organisation has been disbanded, then it cannot be recreated as an alternative. In some very large contracts the procurement of an alternative may be difficult – especially at short notice and at a time when there is substantial demand for services from other local authorities simultaneously on the same track. If such situations exist local authorities may wish to consider dividing their contract into two or more parts, thus ensuring that a practical alternative exists. Such a step would institutionalise an element of competition on performance within the area of the local authority itself – clearly no bad thing.

## 5   BENEFITS FROM CAPITAL SPENDING

Contract conditions should contemplate explicitly the incidence of capital spending during the term of the contract. If, for example, a leisure centre is to be transferred under licence to a management company the agreement must decide how capital improvements are to be financed. In some cases difficult decisions may be necessary. The local council will probably have undertaken to keep the building safe and in good structural repair. If, though, rewiring becomes necessary during the course of the contract there will almost certainly be an element of improvement. No one would contemplate rewiring to a specification of the 1950s. Savings may arise from the installation of new heating equipment or the alterations may simply make the establishment more attractive and, therefore, in theory more profitable. The agreement should describe, at least in principle, how such matters are to be treated.

## 6  VARIATIONS

Variations will undoubtedly be necessary during the contract period. The contract must make provision for this and specify rates at which additional works must be charged or a means of deciding these rates if they cannot be specified. Contractors must have an obligation to meet variations: life would be impossible for the local authority if contractors were put in a position of being able to decline instructions to provide additional or different services.

An alternative form of variation is that which provides savings. For example, the introduction by the contractor of high payload vehicles could reduce refuse collection rounds, giving high windfall savings to the contractor if no contractual provision is made to the contrary. No contract can contemplate every such possibility: but a general provision allowing the local authority to share in such savings is very desirable.

## 7  PRICING POLICIES

The agreement must be clear on the latitude afforded to the contractor on pricing policy. Should the local authority retain a general control; or make a payment to subsidise certain groups such as the old? Or will the contractor be restricted in the price he can charge to these groups throughout the contract? The Council will almost certainly wish to preserve the rights of certain groups (such as schools) to use facilities. There will be a trade off between the financial arrangements following from local management of schools and the charges made by a leisure centre contractor. Full economic pricing may drive away schools, increasing the overall cost to the local authority. Lower prices insisted on in the contract will depress the contractual terms.

There must be a clear contemplation of the position of special interest groups such as this in drawing up the terms of the contract. If not the Council may be propelled into protecting such groups expensively by having to negotiate variations to the contract.

## 8  COMPLAINTS

The contract should specify procedures on complaints from members of the public. Complaints arise now in the delivery of every service to the public by a local authority. They will no doubt continue after contracting out. Since the buck stops with the local authority, complaints will be a thorn in the flesh of Councils unless specific arrangements ar made to cope with them. It will be sensible for the contractor to warrant to deal with complaints at first instance, responsibly, quickly and courteously. Contractors may be required to respond within, say, 24 hours. It would be very desirable for the contractor also to be required to keep a record of complaints, showing how each had been dealt with. It is, after all, to the councillors and the Council that the public will look if their expectations on service delivery are not satisfied.

## 9  RESIDUAL LIABILITY OF THE COUNCIL

Contracting out a service will not relieve a local authority from taking steps to ensure that health and safety standards are observed. It can evaluate the performance both of contractor and direct labour organisation in relation to management systems, health and safety record, information to and qualifications of employees and the health and safety standards to be achieved. Failure to take steps to ensure a reasonable standard of health and safety could put a local authority in breach of criminal law.

## Contract compliance

An increasing number of local authorities have come to see their contracting arrangements as a means of influencing local employment policies. Through contract compliance units and provisions they have sought to ensure that contractors operated full equal opportunities policies; employed a proper number of disabled people; or employed local labour in the execution of contracts. Such practices appear to be outlawed by the Local Government Act, 1988, with the exception of the putting to the contractor of certain 'approved questions', set by the Secretary of State for the Environment.

In debates during the course of the Bill the Government were quite explicit about their intentions to stop contracts compliance practices. Lord Belstead said:

> Part II of the Bill aims to prevent the use of what it describes as 'non-commercial considerations' in contracts and tender lists. It has to be said that these provisions have their origin in quite gross abuses by a number of authorities aimed, for the most part, not at lofty ideals of racial and sexual equality, training or employment of local labour, but simply at deterring private companies from competing with Direct Labour Organisations (Hansard, 16 February 1988).

The Secretary of State for the Environment made it clear that local authorities will be able to ask written questions about race relations practices in pursuance of their duty under Section 71(a) and (b) of the Race Relations Act 1976:

> but only if such questions are in a form that is specified by the Secretary of State.
> Authorities would be allowed to take account of the answers to questions in exercising their contractual functions prior to entering into the contract, but they would not be able to terminate a contract on race relations grounds. By specifying the questions to be asked, we shall enable authorities to fulfil their duties without imposing too excessive a burden on contractors, who, until now, have been faced with different questionnaires from different authorities. Some questionnaires have been extremely long and gone into quite unreasonable detail (Hansard, 14 December 1987).

Following enactment of the legislation, one local authority sought the advice of Leading Counsel on the impact of the Act on their existing contract compliance policy. The opinions they received conflicted with the Government's interpretation of the Act. Counsel advised that local authorities were still free to enquire about a company's behaviour with regard to the Sex

Discrimination Act, 1975, and the Disabled Persons (Employment) Act 1944, and to withhold admission to their approved lists, or to decline to enter into a particular contract if not satisfied with the answers. So far as race relations matters are concerned, Counsel's opinion was that local authorities could continue to do much of what they used to do before the Local Government Act.

Clearly the Government's advice and that given to the local authority are at odds. Any local authority wishing to use contracts in a way beyond that specified by the Secretary of State should take legal advice before doing so.

## Private enhancement of Council contracts

Contracting out is likely to lead to one further consequential change in the nature of the provision of local government services. Local authorities will have contracts for delivery of services to a precise specification at a precise cost. This will make it easier for – and indeed may prompt – some ratepayers to seek a higher specification for some services and be prepared to pay the cost. Already commercial ratepayers in South Molton Street and St Christopher's Place in Westminster pay a charge to the Council to secure a higher standard of street cleansing in their streets. At least one other commercial ratepayer is exploring the possibility of seeking a higher specification. Owners of local shops may well be prepared to pay more for a better or more frequent standard of cleansing. The same principle applies to other services.

The introduction of a national non-domestic rate may speed this process. Local authorities will still, of course, retain interest in the environment and attractiveness of their commercial centres and industrial estates. Nevertheless the severance of the direct link between the provision of services and the amount of the local commercial rate may prompt local authorities to seek extra contributions – especially when marginal expenditure will fall directly on the community charge payer. The principle is, of course, capable of much greater expansion, especially in authorities with a commitment to direct charging as opposed to bearing expenditure through the community charge. It may become the norm for authorities to deliver a standard level of service but for residents to contract directly with a contractor for a higher standard – e.g. more frequent or more convenient refuse collection.

## Conclusion

Contracting out of services will change the way of life of local authorities. It will not free them from their basic statutory responsibilities. In the words of the Local Government Training Board:

> Some have predicted a future for local government in which the elected members meet once a year to give out the contracts. This is a fantasy. Councillors and the Council carry major responsibilities which still have to be exercised. The award of a contract does not remove all responsibility for that activity. The local authority will still bear all its statutory responsibilities. The issue is how those responsibilities should be exercised. The point is that they cannot be exercised as they have been in the past. The constraints imposed by competitive tendering will change the role and activities of the elected members. Failure to realise this will lead to frustration for both officer and member (Local Government Training Board *Councillors and Competition* 1988).

## Using this chapter

▲ *How realistic is your Council's specification? Does it represent actual present standards – or merely aspirations?*

▲ *Does the specification include qualitative as well as quantitative outputs? Are the examples quoted relevant to your service? (1)*

▲ *Have you retained professional expertise sufficient to maintain an adequate inspection service together with capacity to plan ahead? (2)*

▲ *Will there still be a realistic opportunity for competition at the end of the contract period? Or has the Council inadvertently locked itself into one contractor? (3)*

▲ *Is there a ready alternative source if a contractor fails during the contract period? (4)*

▲ *Will the Council share in benefits from improvements to the infrastructure through capital spending? (5)*

▲ *Can the Council easily vary the contract at agreed prices? Will it share in windfall gains? (6)*

▲ *Have you thought through the side-effects of a pricing policy? (7)*

▲ *Will public complaints be speedily dealt with? (8)*

▲ *Is the Council adequately protected against criminal liability? (9)*

▲ *Has the Council given a choice of specification to users with direct charging for enhancement?*

# 4 Partial control: the arm's length agency

**Key points**

▲ *Both voluntarily and by compulsion local authorities are operating more through arm's length agencies*

▲ *Arm's length agencies have separate statutory responsibilities and may have objectives and priorities which diverge from those of the local authority*

▲ *Local authorities should be conscious of the differences between a Council department and an arm's length agency and work to overcome the constraints of relationships*

▲ *Local authorities can influence such relationships positively through joint policy development, joint implementation teams, exchange of staff and mutual support*

▲ *Positive relationships can also be cemented by the sensitive use of more formal mechanisms: statutory powers, finance, representation*

▲ *Public opinion can also be used to influence arm's length agencies*

▲ *Growth of arm's length agencies*

Arm's length agencies under the partial control of the local authority share three features:

▽ They are wholly or largely financed by the local authority.

▽ Members, officers or nominees of the local authority constitute or are represented on the agency.

▽ The agency itself has independent statutory or *de facto* powers.

Arm's length agencies are cuckoos in the nest of local government, serving two masters. Firmly within the local authority ambit, they are wholly or partly immune from local authority control but their interdependence with the local authority gives great scope for influence.

Some are of long standing. Outside Greater London and a small part of the home counties, the Police Service has a long standing statutory background of tripartite control by the Home Secretary, the Police Committee and the Chief Constable. Voluntary schools have a not dissimilar division of responsibilities which can be quadripartite between Government, local authority, diocesan board and governors. Each party has relevant powers spelt out in statute.

Newer categories of arm's length agencies have mushroomed in the last decade. In most cases they are companies created voluntarily by the local authority for a variety of purposes: economic development, ITEC/training, theatres, conservation, sports. Some have been created compulsorily, to run public transport through the Transport Act 1985 and to control local authority airports through the Airports Act 1986.

There is now a new type of relationship, as yet barely recognised by local government: the investing by statute of individual local authority officers with specific statutory responsibilities for which they are directly and personally accountable. So the Treasurer is no longer responsible entirely to the local authority. The latter must reckon on his independent statutory duty in respect of which he can, if necessary, have recourse to the Secretary of State for the Environment.

## Types of arm's length agency

### (a) THE STATUTORY PARTITION OF RESPONSIBILITY

*Police*

The Police Act 1964 specifies the relative duties of Home Secretary, Police Committees (or combined Police Authority) and Chief Constable. Outside the Greater London metropolitan area the Home Secretary is responsible for the overall efficiency of the service; approves each local establishment and appointments of senior officers; and must approve provision of Police buildings within the Home Secretary's approval. The Police Committee must secure the maintenance of an adequate and efficient Police Force; determine the establishment; provide buildings; and appoint senior officers. The County Council (or Councils in the case of combined authorities) as parent authority finances the Police Service with a matching grant from the Home Secretary. The Chief Constable appoints junior officers and controls the deployment of the Police Force. His discretion on operational matters is total. There is considerable inter-working between the Police and the departments of the County Council that provide specialist services: accountancy, legal, architectural, valuation. The Clerk or Secretary of the County Council (or one of the constituent County Councils in the case of a combined Police authority) is commonly the Clerk of the Police Committee and in a position to advise its members. Though only two-thirds of the members of a Police Committee are members of the County Council (the others being drawn from the magistracy), County Councils have often ensured that the majority party on the County Council has also an overall majority on the Police Committee.

Despite the apparent closeness of this relationship, there have been frequent and well publicised differences between Police Committee and Chief Constable. Police Committees have been unsuccessful in attempts to influence Chief Constables on issues like intervention in the miners' strike and the acquisition of plastic bullets. The ill will generated in political *causes celebres* has inhibited collaboration between Police and local authority in less controversial areas. County Councils through their Police Committees have tried to influence overall policing priorities to reflect the perceived anxieties of residents. The willingness of Chief Constables to accept such guidance varies, often in relation to the cordiality of the relationship with the Police Committee. As a Police Force tries to move from being a reactive agency to one which works to specific objectives, there is an increasing role for the Police Committee as representative of the local community to influence the targeting by the Police of their manpower.

*Educational institutions*

The voluntary school sector has shared many of the characteristics of the Police Force. Although funded by the local authority, the governors of the voluntary aided schools are responsible for buildings (other than internal repairs), the use of the school premises, religious instruction and admissions policy. The Education Reform Act 1988 greatly extends the independence of school and college governors, headteachers and principals in both the voluntary and controlled sectors. Some schools may leave the local authority nest entirely by becoming grant-maintained schools. By 1994 every local authority must have brought in a local management scheme which will delegate almost total responsibility for running all but the smallest colleges of further education, all secondary schools and primary schools with more than 200 pupils. There will be a formulaic distribution of budget to institutions.

Thus resources allocated on the basis of the numbers of pupils weighted by age should account for at least 75% of the total schools budget of the local authority. The governors will have discretion over spending of the sum allocated, subject to the power of the local authority to retain not more than 7–10% of the general schools budget for certain specified excepted items.

The effect of the delegation will be to limit the powers of the local authority to determine the total resources available; monitor the performance of schools; and support governing bodies and teachers with professional advice and guidance. Local authorities will continue to plan further education and set the framework within which governing bodies of schools will exercise their delegated powers. Subject to this, schools and colleges within the Act will become substantially independent in the way they interpret the national curriculum, provide courses to students and spend their budgetary allocation. Though local authorities will appoint governors to colleges and schools, they will be in a minority. Already some Councils have decided to appoint governors only from the majority party in order to exercise as great an influence as possible over the ethos of their educational institutions. Such exercises seem to have been counter-productive by promoting anti-local authority member alliances among the other governors.

## (b)   THE VOLUNTARY PARTITION OF RESPONSIBILITY

It is always possible for a local authority to surrender voluntarily part of its functions to a third party with an independent discretion. Such steps have rarely been taken in the past: the ideology of the all-embracing corporate local authority militates against it. The concept of the enabling local authority and the focus on the customer revives the possibility, especially in areas where the local authority's direct management has not been conspicuously successful. The current emphasis on such voluntary divesting of power is in the field of housing management, though there are examples in other areas like leisure centre management. In both the hope is that tenant or customer power may overcome the drawbacks of monolithic centralised estate management. Some Councils are considering transferring ownership of estates to tenant co-operatives. Less radically it is possible for the authority to retain ownership of the estate, but surrender all or part of its management responsibilities to a tenants' committee.

Although there is little experience of substantial tenant management, it is possible to enunciate some of the principles which should apply:

▽ The limits of autonomy should be clearly spelt out and not modified arbitrarily by the Council as circumstances make convenient. The estate management committee should clearly understand their responsibilities, or the scheme will be speedily discredited. Councils should recognise the political stress this may sometimes cause.

▽ The tenants themselves should play a major part in deciding the responsibilities they are to accept.

▽ The local authority should decide at the outset what powers it wishes to retain – allocations policy, for example. It should specify what Council services the tenant's committee must accept and in what areas they are free to choose.

▽ The local authority should retain the ability to monitor the performance of the tenants' committee: not just in its effectiveness, but also in areas key to the local authority's strategy and concerns – care for the elderly and discrimination are examples.

▽ The local authority should retain the capacity to support the tenants' committee where necessary. In particular it must ensure easy liaison with other Council departments. Many of the tenants' concerns will relate to matters outside their scope, e.g. law enforcement, planning, litter and refuse collection.

## (c)   LOCAL AUTHORITY COMPANIES

Local authorities have established companies for three main reasons:

▽ The companies can operate in areas beyond the powers of the local authority, e.g. by the taking of equity shares in other companies.

▽ The companies can raise money from the City without affecting in any way the local authority's own financial regime.

▽ The companies offer a speedier and more confidential form of decision taking than the traditional local authority procedure.

The formation of a company can be effected under Section III of the Local Government Act 1972, which allows authorities to do things which will facilitate or are conducive or incidental to the discharge of their functions. The powers of the company are limited only by its Memorandum of Association. Most companies are limited by guarantee, with guarantees of a nominal amount given by individual councillors or council officers. The companies are normally funded, at least initially, by the local authority. A number of large scale enterprise boards have been created, including the Greater London Enterprise Board, the Greater Manchester Economic Development Corporation, the Kent County Council Enterprise Board, Lancashire Enterprise Limited, the Merseyside Enterprise Board, West Midlands Enterprise and West Yorkshire Enterprises. Most of the boards have created subsidiary companies and have enhanced their original direct investment by additional funds either by loan or investment from the private sector.

The Government consultation paper published in 1988 (Local Authorities' Interests in Companies) promises legislation which would remove much of the point of similar future local authority companies. Broadly the paper proposes bringing such companies within the financial regime of the parent local authority, including treating their capital transactions as if they were transactions by the local authority, restricting the companies' activities to areas where the authority itself has statutory powers, extending compulsory competition to company activities and empowering the local authority Ombudsman to investigate the actions of the companies.

The Transport Act 1985 and the Airports Act 1986 operated to transfer local authority transport undertakings and airports to the control of companies, subject to a wide ranging set of controls laid down in the statutes. At the time the companies were specifically established by the Government as arm's length companies, though paradoxically they fall outside such a definition in the Government's consultation paper, the effect of which would be to lock the airport and public transport companies into the local government finance system.

## (d)  THE INDEPENDENT DUTIES OF OFFICERS OF THE COUNCIL

### Direct labour organisations

The procedures for compulsory competitive tendering attempt to ensure fairness of treatment between outside tenderers and the inside direct labour organisation. It follows that the internal direct labour organisation will also seek equality of treatment with external contractors. This will have substantial internal organisational consequences for local authorities. The conventional wisdom requires that a Chinese wall must divide a direct labour organisation winning a contract from its client body. Separate departments and committees are canvassed.

If direct labour organisations are to be put in the same position as outside tenderers, then they will seek reciprocal advantages: freedom from central bureaucracy, freedom from budgetary, personnel and purchasing restraints. Certainly DLOs will wish to avoid substantial central charges, prompting a re-examination of the role of central departments. Successful DLOs may well be prepared to pay a premium for outside services which are quick and constructive. In its turn this may prompt the central service departments (accountancy, law, valuation, architecture, surveying, purchasing, personnel) to seek freedom from constraints and flexibility in providing a service if they are to compete professionally for the custom of the direct labour organisations. Running a direct fee charging system, they could effectively become mini-direct labour organisations in their own right.

### Separate statutory powers for officers

Apart from the new status of direct labour organisations arising from the legislation on competitive tendering, the most significant development in the law of relationships between Councils and their officers is the conferment by the Local Government Finance Act 1988 of direct independent responsibilities on the Treasurer. He has a statutory duty to report to the Council if it seems that budgets will not balance. He has a duty to collect the community charge; if the Council does not allocate to him the resources he requires then the Secretary of State can adjudicate on the disagreement. Apart from the new power of the Secretary of State, the statutory requirements probably reflect no more than the Treasurer would have conceived as his professional duty. Nevertheless they represent an important constitutional shift. A chief officer employed by the local authority is invested with direct statutory powers regardless of the will of his employing Council. This changes the relationship of employer and employee to a degree which may prove increasingly significant.

Further similar changes to the law were proposed in the Government's response (1988) to the Widdicombe Committee of Inquiry into the conduct of local authority business (1986). The Government proposed:

> In the interests of improving internal accountability and reinforcing the observance of proper procedures to require local authorities to designate an officer to be responsible for propriety generally. He will be responsible for keeping under review the lawfulness and propriety of the Council's activities and reporting to the Council any action or inaction likely to result in:
> (a) An unlawful act;
> (b) A failure to comply with a legal duty;
> (c) Injustice to an individual through maladministration; or
> (d) A departure from the provision of a code of recommended practice where the Council was required to take the code into account.

The officer would have the right of access to information held by the Council and the right to report to the Council as he thought fit.

The Government also proposed:

> That each local authority should be required to designate a single officer to advise the Council on:
> (a) The co-ordination of its various functions;
> (b) The organisation needed to discharge its functions;
> (c) The arrangements needed to ensure proper staffing of that structure.

These proposals are enshrined in the 1989 Local Government and Housing legislation.

Thus three separate statutory duties are imposed upon employees of a local council. The officer responsible for finance may not also be the officer responsible for propriety. The consultation paper envisages 'checks and balances' within the management of the local authority. If there is conflicting opinion and advice, the matter 'should be capable of resolution through discussion and consultation, or by independent legal advice'.

It will obviously be unusual for a local authority to seek independent advice about the activities of one of its own officers. Effectively it puts the officer in the position of a third party, an outside agency with whom the local authority must deal at arm's length. Such situations will, of course, be rare. Their prospect will, nevertheless, change relationships. Indeed Councils may be prompted to adopt a management structure proposed by some to the Widdicombe Committee: an independent secretariat responsible to the Council as a whole and headed by the probity officer; and a separate bureaucracy headed by the management officer with responsibility to the majority party. Such a structure would avoid the conflicts of interest which dual roles entail. It would also avoid the problem of an officer losing the confidence of the majority party through his independent 'probity' role.

## Common approaches

In considering how to relate to agencies under their partial control, an authority must not assume that they can be given instructions – at least not in relation to those areas where there is an independent responsibility. There are, however, a variety of common approaches which can be used by the authority in seeking to influence agencies exercising independent powers.

## 1  PERSONAL RELATIONS

The examples of partial control described above have inevitably concentrated upon the independence of the agencies concerned. It is important that local authorities recognise this. Those involved are not free agents and cannot be prepared to accept the authoritarian bidding of the local authority. In some cases new legislation will have changed relationships formerly taken for granted.

Nevertheless it is misleading to consider the relationships involved as being at arm's length in anything other than a metaphoric sense. The actors concerned have a close daily relationship. The Chairman of the Police Committee and the Chief Constable meet frequently. School inspectors have a regular relationship with headteachers. The directors of a local authority company are the key members or officers of the local authority itself. Officers with an independent statutory responsibility are for a majority of their time subject to direct instruction from the local authority.

Close and friendly personal relationships can overcome many of the problems which would otherwise be encountered. But if a pompous and self-important Chairman of the Police Committee meets a pompous and self-important Chief Constable there will be a clash which with more flexibility could be avoided. In such circumstances the role of the Chief Executive becomes vital: it is his function to smooth ruffled feathers and create a jointly acceptable way forward. Similar functions must be assumed by other local authority chief officers, e.g. the Chief Education Officer in avoiding trials of strength between newly independent headteachers and school inspectors.

## 2  JOINT WORK IN THE DEVELOPMENT OF POLICY

Joint work in the development of policy will avoid clashes. Through a joint approach to the issues a common understanding will be reached. Where common goals are established then the relative parts of the actors become easily defined. Each settles into the role allocated. It is, for example, common for officers of enterprise companies to work closely with officers of a parent local authority in devising for the enterprise board a strategy which meets the authority's objectives. The decisions of enterprise boards may well be considered by local authority committees, emphasising the closeness of the organisations.

Thus in the West Yorkshire Metropolitan County Council there were regular fortnightly meetings between relevant members of the County Council, officers of the Passenger Transport Executive and officers of the County Council in order to thrash out joint approaches to policy. Although the PTE was an agency at arm's length from the County Council, the joint development of policy avoided conflicts which arose elsewhere. As Police Forces increasingly recognise the importance of community policing, joint approaches to sort out priorities have been developed with local authorities. Realising that they need the support of the local authority services to contain crime, joint action becomes not only possible but readily agreed. Moreover the operational necessity of joint collaboration promps close working relation-ships. The traffic division of a Police Force must work closely with the local authority's highways department; drugs abuse can be tackled effectively only by multi-agency collaboration, including the local authority's social services department; crime prevention requires a major input from the local authority. Development of operational links can strengthen joint understanding and minimise the possibility of policy disagreements.

The most dramatic example of the consequences of failure to work through policy jointly (even when not technically at arm's length) between the different actors is contained in the former Greater London Council's 'fares fair' policy.

When the original Labour Party manifesto commitment to cheap fares was overturned by the House of Lords, great confusion resulted. What had the Greater London Council to do to relieve itself from a potential breach of the law and surcharge for its members? The Secretary of State for Transport had advice that a 60 % increase in fares, restoring the *status quo ante* plus inflation, would comply with the law. The GLC and London Transport officers had different legal advice. They put forward a package which would double fares and canvassed the need for further increases later. When Tory members of the Greater London Council moved increases in accordance with the Secretary of State's views, the GLC Director-General warned that such a move could put the Council in breach of its statutory duty. The adoption of the officers' recommendations came after scenes of great chaos and confusion.

## 3  SUPPORT TO THE AGENCIES

None of the agencies is an island; each one is a piece of the whole, a part of the main. Each relies upon support from the local authority. The more willingly and graciously the support is offered, the more willingly will the agency cleave to the authority's priorities and policies. Schools, for example, are greatly influenced by local authority inspectors, who themselves take instruction directly from the local authority. The inspectors represent professional expertise and schools disregarding their advice may well feel that they do so at their peril. Although, therefore, a school governing body could modify the local authority's curriculum, there may well be great reluctance to do so if it imperils the relationship with the inspector. Governors may well have the right to choose a principal or a teacher; but could be reluctant to disregard the firm advice of the local authority's education officer, a person of direct professional expertise. At best his advice would be welcome; at worst governors could fear the consequences of disregarding his advice being firmly visited upon their heads (and Heads). Local authority companies often do not have the comprehensive knowledge which they need to cope adequately with their responsibilities: they need an input from the local authority traffic engineers, planners and demographic experts. All these avenues present opportunities for influence.

Nor is support only logistical. A Police Force may need routine help from a local authority: the erection of barriers, the pruning of trees, the closure of roads. But a Chief Constable also needs support from the Council as spokesman for the local community. If wheelclamping is under attack, it is a great benefit to receive support from the local Council. Such support is likely to increase the willingness of the Police to follow the local authority's priorities, whether it be the control of street prostitution, better enforcement of coach routeing or stopping litter louts. Equally an officer of the Council relies upon the collaboration of his colleagues and members of the Council. He will dislike taking action which reduces the support he receives from them.

Schools which have opted for grant-maintained status have almost total independence. Yet even here the local authority retains certain powers and duties: the provision of a careers service and provision for pupils with special educational needs are examples. There will be a temptation for a local authority to wash its hands of a grant-maintained school. Yet the school remains part of the educational resource in the area; the Council will take its provision into account in its overall planning. If the Council wishes to retain an influence, then it could offer its advisory services to this school on payment. Its in-service training could also be offered, ensuring a continued relationship between teachers in the school and local authority schools.

## 4   INTERNAL TRACKING

A local authority can set-up its own internal unit to 'track' the external agency. A unit designed to second-guess an agency may well be seen to arouse resentment. Undoubtedly this will be the first reaction. However such a unit would acquire an expertise in the area of the agency which will make it appreciate the problems. It may not be realistic to expect an authority to appoint an officer to second-guess the Treasurer; but this is undoubtedly what would happen in the case of substantial conflict. But a unit within the authority to advise it on transport or airport operations would enable the authority's representative members to be better informed and have a more realistic expectation of what could in practice be done. If policing priorities are an issue, then an internal unit which can articulate rational criteria may well be welcomed by the Police – more than the random priorities of different councillors. The authority will in any case have a substantial unit able to track schools and advise on their performance.

Such units will have a relationship with the agency concerned which can promote better understanding with the Council. Anybody is better able to react constructively to informed and articulated comment. The members of an Enterprise Board, receiving advice from its officers on complicated financial matters with which they may have no familiarity, will be much better able to exert control if they receive proper briefing from local authority employees. In turn the employees of the enterprise board will be more accountable.

Debate in a Police Committee will be better informed if members have before them an independent analysis of crime trends. The nearest analogy is that of the Home Secretary. As Police Authority for Greater London, the Home Secretary stands in relation to the Metropolitan Police as a Police Committee does to a provincial Police Force. The Home Secretary has in the Home Office a unit with the responsibility of tracking the Metropolitan Police, its finances, efficiency and priorities. Why should a Police Committee not have the same facility if the local authority has as a priority the influencing of the Police Force?

## 5  JOINT STAFFING ARRANGEMENTS

Long term, the understanding between agencies can be greatly enhanced if their staffs have a mutually shared experience. This can be achieved by secondment to an agency by the local authority, or vice versa. In some cases job swaps may be possible. In many cases there is every reason to seek joint training arrangements. If management development programmes are being organised by the local authority for its managers, every possible effort should be made to ensure that officers of the arm's length agencies, such as policemen, attend and share the experience. Such activities will not produce overnight results. But in the long term they will ensure that understanding, sharing and knowledge of cultures which is crucial to collaborative working.

## 6  THE FULL USE OF STATUTORY POWERS

A local authority usually has some sort of statutory powers over the arm's length agency. For example, the Chief Constable may be asked by the Police Committee to:

▽  submit a report to it on matters connected with policing the area;
▽  report on the state of crime, how the force is deployed and on major incidents which have given rise to complaint;
▽  report on the extent of police protection in a particular area.

The Police Committee is a forum for exchanging views on policing issues, policies and priorities. Members can assess the effectiveness of the Police Force through use of their powers. When complaint has arisen about the inability of Police Committees to influence Chief Constables, a common reply has been that these powers have been seldom exercised. Many Chief Constables would, indeed, welcome their exercise and take steps to promote discussion of policing issues. Often the absence of a brief to local authority members has prevented matters being taken up in a constructive way.

Equally if a development company is a creature of the local authority, it may have set for it precise objectives and criteria to which it must perform. If such objectives are not set, Councils can hardly complain that they have no control over the outcome. Information can be required from passenger transport companies which can inform the debate by the local authority and enable it to exercise effective control.

## 7  REPRESENTATION

The representatives of the local authority on an arm's length agency are a means of exercising control. Too often local authorities show their belief in the Thomas à Becket syndrome: when appointed the representative 'goes native' and joins the forces of the body to which he or she is appointed. Local council representatives on a school governing body clearly can be influential. So can members of the Police Committee. Even more so can be members of the companies controlled by a majority of councillors.

One simple device is to ensure reporting back. The Government, in its consultation paper on local authority's interests in companies, says:

There is an inevitable risk that, without specific provisions to ensure access to information, councillors will not be kept in touch with the company's affairs. It is desirable therefore to introduce requirements to ensure that:

(a) The local authority is kept informed of any business which is to come before a company meeting;
(b) It may issue instructions to the representative which he is bound to follow.

The requirement to report back and account for these activities can be a salutory discipline for all representative members; help to maintain the flow of information; and ensure accountability.

## 8   FINANCE

The local authority controls the purse strings of these arm's length agencies. A local authority company depends largely upon the local authority for its continuing funding. The local authority enjoys a total discretion in that case. Even in the case of schools, where discretionary spending may be as little as 7%, a local authority still retains a lever. In its control of capital spending a local education authority has an ability to offer sought benefits to the school. It may be unrealistic or undesirable to expect this mechanism to be used as blackmail. Nevertheless control of the residual budget gives a Council an opportunity for asserting its own priorities. Elements of a police budget may be seen as inessential by the Police Committee. School budgets can be constructed so as to give a bias, for example, towards community use – something which might otherwise be neglected by governing bodies and headteachers, with a single minded commitment to education only. Specific budgets set aside for a purpose close to the local authority's heart can be very effective.

## 9   THE COMMUNITY

The local authority as a conduit for community choice can ensure that the community receives full information about the services available to it. Published comparative statistics on school performance can not only fulfil a function in relation to the community; it can also influence the behaviour of schools themselves. The statutory Police Consultative Groups can form another avenue through which local authority members can exert pressure on local policing priorities.

## 10   PUBLICITY

A local authority has great access to publicity. It knows the municipal reporters, who take an interest in its doings. It will probably have a public relations officer or unit which can activate the local press. If such facilities are to be used to arouse outright hostility towards an agency, then they will probably be counter-productive. However if a local authority, having articulated clearly its own policies and priorities, uses its access to the media to create a climate of opinion to which agencies must respond, then that is a different matter. If a local council genuinely articulates public concern then the press will reflect that concern. It is not for long that an agency can resist such pressures. Indeed the agency may welcome such media interest as a means of gauging public opinion and validating its own priorities.

## 11   THE THREAT OF STATUTORY REDRESS

If all these fail there are usually statutory redresses. The delegation scheme to a school can be withdrawn, subject to appeal to the Secretary of State. The dismissal of the Chief Constable can be sought from the Home Secretary. A local authority company can be wound up. The Treasurer can be dismissed. All these remedies reflect failure and can be used only where relationships have deteriorated to impossibility; and where, moreover, the blame lies almost exclusively with the agency itself. Every local authority must labour constructively and hard to ensure that these situations are not encountered.

# Conclusion

In the new world of arm's length agencies, the onus lies on the local authority (as well as on the agency) to ensure that constructive steps are taken to ensure that relationships succeed. Both local authority and agency require each other in a collaborative attack on their mutual problems.

Statutes may specify a separation of powers. But if close working relationships are established this formal separation may serve as no more than a backcloth to the informal relationships which are needed for the effective governance of the area.

## Using this chapter

▲  *Have you considered the independent discretion of the arm's length agencies through which your Council operates? Have you considered the effect of the recent statutory changes on these relationships? Have you modified your organisation as a result?*

▲  *Have the independent statutory powers given to, or to be given to, officers of the Council prompted the Council to review its management structure?*

▲  *Do you recognise the independence of the actors involved and seek positive steps to maintain close personal relationships? (1)*

▲  *With which arm's length agencies do you have joint policy teams? With which others should joint policy development arrangements be made? (2)*

▲  *Do you use support to agencies as a conscious method of influence? (3)*

▲  *Do you monitor systematically the work of arm's length agencies? Do you provide the local authority's representatives with an independent source of advice to enable them to make a positive contribution to the agency? (4)*

▲  *What arrangements do you have to share experience between staff of the agency and staff of the local authority? (5)*

▲  *Do you brief councillors on the extent of the powers available to them in relation to arm's length agencies? Are those powers fully used? (6)*

▲  *Are local authority representatives on arm's length agencies briefed as to their role? Or on the local authority's policies? Are those policies clearly articulated? (7)*

▲  *Is the finance afforded to arm's length agencies where possible tied to the local authority's priorities? (8)*

▲  *Does the local authority makes the community aware of the activities of the arm's length agencies? (9)*

▲ *Does the local authority give publicity to the activities of the agencies? Does*
  *it seek to inform consumer choice and thus influence the agencies? (10)*
▲ *Are you aware of the statutory powers the authority possesses in relation to the*
  *agency? (11)*

# 5 Partnership: joint operations

## Key points

▲ *Local authorities will continue to search for and work with partners in tackling the problems of their areas*
▲ *Such partnerships work smoothly only where there is a genuine community of interest of the partners*
▲ *Local authorities must recognise the problems which inhibit successful partnerships and take steps to overcome them*
▲ *Factors which help partnerships achieve:*

   ▽ *clarity and modesty of aim*
   ▽ *co-terminosity*
   ▽ *establishment of key tasks or rewards*
   ▽ *co-option to local authority committees or steering groups*
   ▽ *middle management commitment*
   ▽ *the right machinery*
   ▽ *the quick trick and the flagship*
   ▽ *the injection of resources*
   ▽ *the right skills*
   ▽ *sharing of power*
   ▽ *pooling of data*
   ▽ *one boss*

## Definition

Partial control is a situation where the local authority has control over some but not all of the actions of an agency. Partnership, on the other hand, is a relationship between the local authority and other bodies, where all parties retain constitutional freedom of action but agree to collaborate in pursuit of some joint goal.

## The need for partnership

One of the paradoxes of the fragmentation of services across organisational boundaries is the growing conventional wisdom that joint working is essential.

The Home Office Standing Conference on Crime Prevention (1987) says: 'We believe that there is a need for a systematic inter-agency approach to juvenile crime prevention at the local level'. Similar sentiments have been uniformly expressed by official reports on child abuse, community care and drugs abuse.
    The reasons are:

▽ The need of the consumers, such as the elderly, cross the boundaries of the agencies and professions.
▽ Without joint working there will be gaps in service provision.
▽ Joint working can make better use of resources which would otherwise be wasted in duplicated activity or in less than cost-effective services.
▽ The strategies of different agencies may actually be pulling in different directions and be counter-productive.

The exhortations of official reports have a touching faith in the rationality of inter-organisational planning and working. Unfortunately all experience and research shows that the rational actor planning model is rarely achieved. It is even more difficult to achieve when it has to take place between different agencies with different objectives, different cultures, and often different boundaries. If partnership is to work considerable efforts and adaptations have to be made. The mere existence of a joint planning machinery by no means shows it to be successful in its assumed objectives.
    Despite these problems all parties agree that major problems facing local government – mainly in the inner cities – can be solved only by a partnership of those concerned, including both public and private sector. While much rhetoric surrounds this statement a growing number of local authorities have established inter-agency partnerships, notably involving the private sector. The concept is endorsed by the Confederation of British Industry. British Urban Development, a consortium of eleven construction companies, has launched the concept of Partnership Enterprize Zones, to bring together private and public funding for inner city regeneration. Several major multi-agency task forces, like the Glasgow Eastern Area Renewal Project (GEAR) have achieved great success.

    In their publicity the City of Newcastle-upon-Tyne says: 'Partnership is not a new concept for the City of Newcastle-upon-Tyne. The Grey Street Renaissance is an initiative which exemplifies the spirit of partnership between civic and commercial interests that has prevailed in the City throughout its long history.'

## Local authorities and their partners

Some partnerships are with a single partner: care in the community initiatives with the local health authorities are obvious examples. In other cases a large number of bodies may constitute a forum. The Home Office Standing Conference on Crime Prevention recommends that the local juvenile crime panel should include representatives of the youth service, the local business community, relevant voluntary organisations, young people and their parents as well as police, probation, social services, education and representatives of the magistracy. Where numerous bodies are involved, it is essential that one agency be given responsibility for taking the lead. The push on juvenile crime prevention originally made little progress because of the lack of earmarking of a lead agency. A subsequent leaflet jointly published by NACRO and SOLACE urged chief executive to take the lead. Sometimes the lead partner may not be the most obvious protagonist. Often local authorities like Birmingham are making the running in the WHO-inspired Healthy Cities initiative. Through a joint committee with the public, voluntary and statutory agencies, mechanisms are being created for public participation and debate. Development of health indicators and health status surveys are a priority.

Regeneration of declining cities has prompted some of the more imaginative partnerships:

In Halifax the Calderdale Partnership has been created, set up under the auspices of Business in the Community as a joint venture between public and private sectors. Representation on its steering group is split between the Calderdale District Council, four local businessmen and BIC's Development Director. The partnership has secured a £200 000 revolving loan fund from Rowntree Mackintosh, a local company, to refurbish buildings and sites; a study into Asian community needs sponsored by Northern Foods; establishment of a venture capital office by Hambros Advanced Technology Trust; the creation of a national learning centre for children on a derelict site, with voluntary sector funding; and the loan by Marks and Spencer of management trainees to small Calderdale firms.

In adjoining Kirklees the Council has forged a long-term link with a Yorkshire-based building and civil engineering contractor. Profits from a jointly-owned company will be shared with a proportion ploughed back into desirable but unremunerative projects. The partnership is capable of termination by either side and embraces the possibility of other contractors being employed. It is designed to create and improve housing, commercial, industrial, social and leisure facilities in the area.

## Issues likely to prompt partnerships:

▽   care in the community
▽   regeneration of the inner cities
▽   development or restoration of a town centre
▽   preservation of a tract of countryside
▽   tackling unemployment problems
▽   employment creation
▽   drugs misuse
▽   AIDS
▽   juvenile crime
▽   child abuse
▽   provision of housing
▽   links between business and education

These are examples of partnerships with a long-term strategic aim. Every local authority has a multitude of operational partnerships which are taken for granted in the day-to-day running of the local authority.

## Conditions for success in partnership

Local authorities, like all organisations, seek partnerships when they recognise a problem which they cannot solve within their own organisational boundaries or where they can see advantage by collaboration. Operational collaboration is relatively easy to achieve. Joint working between field officers is common and usually successful provided that there are no inter-personal problems. The community policeman relates to schools; licensing officers work with police on control of sex establishments; refuse collectors have informal arrangements with the private sector for the collection of the latter's rubbish.

Strategic relationships are much more difficult, even when collaborative mechanisms have been created and where common effort is subject to Government exhortation. Care in the community has been the by-word for a quarter of a century, yet progress has been extremely uneven and patchy, partly because of financial constraints, but also because of a lack of genuine shared aims.

> The Government target on mental health services is that National Health Service expenditure should represent 87 % of the total and local authorities 13 %. In 1977 97 % of expenditure was incurred by the health service and 3 % by local authorities. By 1985 National Health Service spending had been reduced only marginally to 95.5 % and local authorities increased only to 4.5 %.

Any formal collaborative machinery – especially if it is set up under statutory compulsion and without genuine commitment by both parties – will fail unless there is joint commitment to sharing a problem. If one of the partners feels that the problem is peripheral to his interests joint working will be unsuccessful:

> In 1965 the GLC was endowed with a research and intelligence function. A planning information system was set up by which the London Boroughs would send a copy of every planning decision together with the original application and site plan to the GLC. The GLC would analyse these and supply quarterly computer reports on the pattern of permissions granted.
>
> The GLC soon lagged behind with processing and complained to the boroughs about inaccurate and late returns. The vast information generated was too much for the boroughs to absorb and its lateness made it increasingly irrelevant. Boroughs began to create their own planning information systems, encouraged by a time lapse of returns from the GLC which grew to two and a half years. The system collapsed because the boroughs did not perceive any genuine advantage to them in its use; and the GLC remained unwilling to simplify it.

A contrasting example is a partnership generated over many years between Pilkington PLC and the St Helens Council.

> Pilkingtons participated in the creation of the Community of St Helens Trust, to provide counselling to small and start-up businesses as long ago as 1978. In 1979 Pilkington encouraged other major local employers to create a source of venture capital to enable the growth of small firms. In 1980 Pilkington established a company to train young people. The

company has now set up a community programme for young unemployed. Pilkingtons have also joined with other employers to form a company to regenerate derelict land in St Helens. The immediate plan is to redevelop a 236 acre site near the town centre.

Pilkingtons totally shared the commitment of the Borough Council to the regeneration of the town. It is relatively unusual to find an employer so tied to one locality. Such a tie clearly generates a commitment. The investment of Pilkingtons in St Helens is similar to that of many American companies to their base. Indianapolis has been largely regenerated by the efforts of Eli Lilly. Commitment on this scale is easier to create where the company operates with both headquarters and work force in the locality. The problem is shared.

The problems of the Cleveland drug abuse case in part stem from the fact that not one of the agencies was prepared to share the entire problem: each dealt with its own part. No synoptic view was taken by any of the participants.

Partners may, though, have a much lower level of interest in the problem than the local authority and yet find a self-interested motive for collaborating constructively. The shrinking numbers of school leavers in the early 1990s will, for example, prompt employers to remedy their skill shortages by collaborating in training ventures in the inner cities where the unemployed will represent a resource which cannot be neglected.

In Gateshead a tele-shopping service has been provided for the housebound and for those who have difficulty in shopping. The service is a joint venture provided by the Gateshead Social Services and Libraries and Arts Departments. These departments work with the local Tesco supermarket, Kays Mail Order and other local suppliers. There is, no doubt, an element of community spirit in the services provided by the private sector. Nevertheless the scheme enables them to fulfil their main objective of selling goods.

Similarly:

Nottinghamshire County Council runs a professional services voucher scheme in conjuction with the Nottingham Society of Chartered Accountants and the Nottingham Law Society. This enables local small firms to receive subsidised advice on issues such as the legal requirements for starting a business, patent work, or taxation up to the value of the voucher.

Provided that a local authority can take a strategic view of the needs of a specific sector, then it can plan services which can be provided by agencies with a narrower sub-objective only.

## Inhibitions on partnership

▽   Organisations which feel vulnerable may be reluctant to surrender some of their powers. This fear characterised the relationship between Metropolitan Districts and Metropolitan Counties before the latter's abolition. If one partner has a specific objective of absorbing functions from the other, then relationships are unlikely to be comfortable and relaxed.

▽    Different cultures and different professional backgrounds hamper under-
     standing. The political culture of a local authority may jar on non-political
     agencies. Anecdotal evidence suggests that councillor members of health
     authorities are treated with caution by their colleagues. It is alleged that
     they do not attend regularly; they are perceived as awkward and difficult
     by other members; they make rhetorical political speeches rather than
     address the issue; and are concerned about their own power base. Coun-
     cillors on the other hand, allege that health authority members with no
     power base are confused as to their role, ineffective, and not prepared to
     take on the General Manager/Chairman coalition. Tensions are evidenced
     by the well publicised removals from Health Authorities, from time to
     time, of local authority members ranging from Mrs Teresa Stewart to Sir
     Jack Smart.
▽    Co-terminosity is by no means a recipe for success. However, absence of
     it can make life difficult for a local authority which has to relate to a
     number of different agencies or agencies which have to cope with a
     number of different local authorities. Often the different priorities of the
     agencies can be further confused by different geographical priorities.
▽    A functional split may prevent agreement on what should be a shared
     overall objective of general welfare. For example during the early days
     of general improvement areas and housing action areas, borough councils
     became frustrated about the reluctance of county councils to make
     available funds for highway improvements, often an essential part of
     improving an area. The county councils regarded their finance as being
     for highway purposes, not for environmental improvements.
▽    In some cases operational relationships may be hindered by different
     working practices. For example joint centres for the under fives, staffed by
     the social services department nursery attendants, education department
     teachers and health authority employees may suffer because of the dif-
     ferent conditions of service of the protagonists. The shorter working
     hours and longer holidays of the teachers distort rational provision,
     forcing arbitrary working practices which have nothing to do with client
     needs.

## How to make partnership work

### 1   CLARITY OF AIM

It is not enough to agree a general objective. Both or all partners must agree
precise aims. If the local authority cannot achieve agreement on the totality
of its objective, then either ambitions must be scaled down or the partnership
aborted.

     The Cleveland Juvenile Crime Group's terms of reference focus on:

▽    establishing an annual review of juvenile justice;
▽    supplying regular statistical analyses of juvenile crime;
▽    instigating and co-ordinating juvenile crime prevention initiatives;
▽    reviewing juvenile liaison and police cautioning;
▽    developing alternatives to custody in care (SOLACE/NACRO 1987).

These objectives are relatively limited (with the exception of the third).

They form a precise framework upon which a group can focus. The professionals involved should have no difficulty in working to such aims. If there are problems on the sharing of major objectives – or even of mutual trust – a way forward may be to establish a group with limited objectives. In this way a successful working climate can be created and can be the bridge to a larger objective. An initially modest aim is more likely to succeed. Joint planning in community care has often foundered because of an attempt to move across all priority groups simultaneously.

Such a method cannot be successful, though, where there is a genuine divergence of aim masked by a common overall objective.

A charitable foundation wished to set up an innovative day centre for the elderly which would combine modern American practice and design with general health care and a research capability for geriatric care in the community. Both health authority and local authority were excited by the prospect and detailed planning followed. It was clear from the outset that the foundation wished to see a day centre of some size: only thus could the scale of provision contemplated be economically justified. The social service department philosophy was totally against large day centres as being institutional. Compromises were consistently reached; but eventually the foundation reviewed the final version of the package. The investment they contemplated could not be justified in view of the small number of places involved. They withdrew from the venture.

In a project-oriented joint venture such as this a genuine meeting of minds is necessary. There will have to be endless compromises over details; but if there is real conflict over the overall aim the project cannot be satisfactorily concluded. At the outset of any project make sure that the participants agree clearly terms of reference and aims. If this exercise discloses general disagreement the whole partnership must be reviewed or its nature changed.

## 2  CO-TERMINOSITY

Much has been written about the issue of co-terminosity (i.e. the sharing of common boundaries) between health authorities and local government. Local authorities have always had a substantial commitment towards co-terminosity – originally with the hope that co-terminosity would simplify bringing the Health Service under local authority control (an original Government aspiration). Latterly local authorities have sought co-terminosity to aid joint planning, notably in the field of community care (though there are other inter-actions between health authority and local authority – environmental health, school health, planning). Health authorities have been less concerned about co-terminosity though research shows that the nearer a health service employee is to community care, then the more concerned he or she will be about co-terminosity. Indeed the research is cited as an example of the way in which the Health Service is dominated by those more concerned with acute services.

There is clearly a problem for a local authority in negotiating partnerships across its area with a multiplicity of partners. On the whole local authorities are centralised in the sense, at least, of central policy formation. It is difficult to adapt policies for different partners giving the same service.

It will remain an aim for the local authorities to achieve co-terminosity with the health service and, no doubt, with other agencies with which it interacts – notably representative bodies like Chambers of Commerce. If this cannot be achieved then the desire for close partnership may prompt the local authority to restructure its own divisions to correspond with those of the partner. So in Westminster the geographical boundaries of decentralised staff have been adjusted to be consistent so as to enable colleagues in different departments readily to work together. However the links between the Social Services Department and Health Authority are closer than, for example, links between social services and housing. Desirable though social services/housing links are, the Social Services Department has been structured to correspond with Health Authority boundaries.

*Ad hoc* groupings may be able to forge similar relationships on a temporary basis by innovative practice: the City of Westminster has established a zone improvement patrol (ZIP) team, a body of multi-purpose inspectors who will blitz an area, using all the battery of the Council's statutory powers. During their well publicised occupation of the area, they are able to start and maintain close relations with the local police station, a closeness which could not be maintained consistently with every police station in the City throughout the year.

> The unlicensed sex industry in Soho has always been a major problem. Its Protean nature frustrated the collective attempts of the Greater London Council, the City of Westminster and the police. Though totally committed to a common objective, the statutory authorities were never a match for the ingenuity of the sex kings. The abolition of the Greater London Council (whatever its other merits and demerits) improved matters enormously. The GLC'c licensing powers were transferred to the City Council, which restructured its own operations so that all licensing and regulatory powers were collected together. With a major concentration of effort on Soho the teams were able to work with the police as a unified force to deploy every statutory power available to them. Although the elimination of one of the partners was a help in achieving consistency of aim, the greater benefit was the tightness and consistency of the area with which the team had to deal, liaising with the local police station to whom the sex industry and associated crime was a major concern.

Co-terminosity helps because it creates the conditions necessary to achieve a commonality of aim. An organisation with a wider geographical area will inevitably be more diffuse in its priorities than one with a narrower area. An organisation with a narrower area may not share the wider strategy of the larger. If joint working and partnership in an area is a priority – and the boundary of the external agency cannot be changed – then the local authority's internal boundaries can be changed to suit the external organisation.

## 3   KEY TASKS AND REWARDS

The day-to-day job of managing an authority's services will often drive out the ability of a Chief Executive or a Chief Officer to devote the time and constructive thought necessary for diplomacy and development of joint schemes with an external agency. Such relationships are extremely time consuming. The Chief Officer shoulders direct blame if his own service declines. He will not be criticised if an external agency does not produce to the Council's satisfaction. The increasing trend of arm's length agencies will operate so as to free some time for Chief Officers: but the day-to-day always drives out the optional and long term.

Performance appraisal systems are becoming increasingly common in local government. Key tasks are set for Chief Officers. Performance is measured. In some authorities successful performance is rewarded by bonus payments. The most easily quantified and established key tasks relate to internal performance. If partnership with an external agency is seen as key to the local authority's holistic strategy for the area, then the key tasks for the Chief Executive and Chief Officers should reflect this.

Of course an independent actor is not controllable. A key task may fail simply because the external agency fails to respond. This does not preclude the setting of such a key task: if it should not be fulfilled the officer can be asked to account for the steps which he has taken and the time devoted to procuring a successful outcome. He can be asked to predict what further steps can be taken, including what pressure can be mounted on the outside organisation to change its stance.

Key tasks can be general: to establish a strategic relationship with the external agency. At its most simple this can be reflected in the number of meetings; more cogently by the agreement of joint objectives; and most specifically by the achievement of certain aims. Even a general aspiration can be covered in key tasks: one Chief Officer has a key task of producing three joint venture schemes each year with external partners.

In key areas an annual review can look at what has been achieved. It can be reported not only to the local authority but also to the other partners or prospective partners in a venture. Released to the press it will play a part in shaping public opinion. The SOLACE/NACRO report *Local Authority Action on Juvenile Crime* (1987) states:

> Each area should have an annual review of juvenile crime. The annual review should include reports on local levels of juvenile crime, prosecution and custodial sentencing, together with reports to the local authority and other agencies on progress to date and future plans. These reports should be put together and published annually by the local authority.

Such a review can form the basis of performance appraisal of the individual local authority protagonists. Other agencies can be persuaded to set similar key tasks for their executives.

## 4   CO-OPTION TO LOCAL AUTHORITY COMMITTEES

Non-executive directors are the private sector equivalent of co-opted members. They are chosen to give independence and expertise to the board of a company, but also sometimes because of the relationship between their main company and the company of which they are non-executive director. The co-option of a representative of a partnership on a local authority committee or working party may be successful in infusing the partner with enthusiasm for the local authority's policy aims. After all local authority members sent as representatives to outside bodies usually become devotees for the outside body. The same may not be true in reverse, especially in political meetings: outsiders tend to be alienated by the adversarial style of local authority committees.

Moreover the success of a venture does depend upon the ability of the co-optee to influence his parent organisation: there is no point in co-opting somebody who will not be able to reflect adequately the local authority's views back to his parent body. The co-option of representatives of, say, the groups which are under-represented on the Council or disadvantaged (e.g. ethnic minorities, women, the business community, disabled people) are unsuccessful viewed in this light: there is no body to whom they can report. Of course a representative of an ethnic minority or a woman may be able to enlarge the deliberations of the committee: but they are not responsible to any constituency.

In future co-options to local authority committees are to be restricted. Partnership in the education field between the local authorities and Church will be enshrined in the compulsory co-option of representatives of Diocesan Boards. Other co-optees will not be able to vote; in other words they will function as advisers. In appropriate cases this need not prevent their taking a full part in the deliberations of the committee, short of voting. Such co-options are most likely to be useful in specifically orientated project groups rather than on main service committees or sub-committees.

## 5   MIDDLE MANAGEMENT COMMITMENT

There is an interesting inability of organisations to interact successfully at middle management level. The most common and also the most successful type of inter-organisational partnership exists at street level. Officers with an operational responsibility perceive clearly those with whom they have to have a relationship if they are to be successful in their task. They work hard to cement the relationship. The commitment to the customer drives practitioners towards collaboration to deliver the services needed. An immediate task orientation simplifies relationships. Of course the success of relationships depends upon the freedom of action of those responsible at street level. The more decentralised the organisation, the more able are street level practitioners to commit resources, change priorities and adjust policy to forge a coalition with other relevant agencies. *If street level collaboration is a necessary part of an authority's strategy, then devolved management is a pre-condition of successful collaboration.*

Those at the top of the organisation equally may find it easy to establish a *rapprochement* with their opposite number in another agency. An Olympian remoteness facilitates macro-planning. Commitment in principle by those at the top of the organisation is, though, not sufficient to activate integrated collaboration. Equally, as Neil McKeganey and David Hunter (1986) put it:

> While joint working at street level perhaps ought to infuse joint planning at higher levels, in practice joint planning appears to proceed independently from activities at street level.

The Butler–Sloss Inquiry into child abuse in Cleveland identified a precisely similar problem: differences of view at middle management level were not recognised by senior staff. These differences eventually affected those working on the ground.

Local authority/police relationships are a frequent example of good collaboration at top and bottom of an organisation, with a yawning void in the middle. The Chief Executive and the Chief Constable find a ready joint commitment to the welfare of the area and joint working on crime prevention. At street level, operational relationships are good: the trading standards officers and other local authority inspectors get ready help from the local police. In their turn the police can get quick and easy assistance from decentralised local authority personnel like the estate housing manager and the headteacher. The problem lies in the middle. There may be an agreement in principle that the local authority will do what it can to encourage crime prevention. Yet planners still design pedestrian precincts which are conducive to crime. The local authority may be most sensitive to illegal parking in a residential area, yet cannot succeed in persuading the police to divert resources accordingly.

It is clearly the function of those at the top to infuse middle management with a clear understanding of the need for partnership. Middle managers may not have the overview obtained by those at the top of the organisation. They are equally remote from service delivery. Nevertheless they set the policies of those below them. Inter-organisational partnerships will founder if middle management do not share a sense of commitment to joint working.

Those at the top of organisations have ready access to each other. Those at the bottom create easy and informal working relationships dictated by operational necessity. If partnership is to be wholehearted, opportunities must be created for middle managers to share ownership of the joint policies by their involvement in the planning processes.

## 6   THE FORMAL MACHINERY OF COLLABORATION

In cases where partnership is seen to be essential and joint working a necessary regular feature, a joint machinery for partnership can be prescribed. In some areas its procedures can be laid down in very precise terms. The formal liaison prescribed by the Butler–Sloss Inquiry is an example. Central child protection registers listing all children who have been abused, or at risk of abuse and subject to an inter-agency plan, should be maintained in every Social Services Department. Five categories are prescribed: neglect, physical abuse, sexual abuse, emotional abuse and grave concern. The purpose of the register is to provide a record of all children in the area who are currently the subject of an inter-agency protection plan and to ensure that the plans are formally received at least every six months. The case conference review will be chaired by a senior member of staff of the Social Services Department or NSPCC who does not have direct involvement in the case. All relevant agencies must be present.

Procedures of such tightly prescribed formality are, of course, unusual. In areas where inter-agency collaboration is vital, such as child abuse, it may be necessary or desirable to prescribe procedures so tightly that problems cannot escape resolution by dropping through interstices between agencies.

The need for shotgun machinery of this sort can be acceptable to protagonists where the consequences of the failure of inter-agency collaboration have become all too obvious. In most cases such rigidity would arouse resentment and impose an unnecessary straight-jacket if collaboration depends upon honest trading. Over-tight prescriptiveness may be counter-productive. The senior management have the responsibility to ensure that machinery does exist through which trading can take place. Long-term success may depend on the extent to which such machinery becomes part of the normal management process.

## 7   THE QUICK TRICK AND THE FLAGSHIP

The fruits of inter-agency collaboration may frequently be intangible or difficult to measure. In other cases there may be a long and discouraging lead time before any tangible results are achieved. The taking of a quick trick can be a great encouragement and spur to the joint venture. A drugs project may, for example, have as its major objective the creation of a residential establishment where women with young children who feel that they are at risk from falling into addiction can go for a short spell to receive mutual and staff support. Such a project, involving at least three agencies and the procurement of substantial resources, is likely to take some time to achieve. While battling to overcome bureaucratic barriers and to wring money from agencies in straitened circumstances, protagonists could be greatly encouraged by some recognition of their joint endeavours. For example, they could be offered a drugs helpline, giving telephone access to advice. Its cost could be minimal and existing staff used to provide the service. Equally sponsorship can readily be found for certain one-off projects. A crime prevention panel could be encouraged by the distribution of a crime prevention handbook, which ought to receive ready sponsorship from insurance companies.

The same psychological encouragement can be derived even more strongly from a flagship. Local authorities are increasingly recognising the potential of up-market arts facilities for publicising the attractions of their areas. Bradford's Alhambra Theatre, the City of Birmingham Symphony Orchestra, and the Glasgow Opera House are examples. If flagships confer status and kudos on entire areas, they can similarly bless partnerships. One of the most striking flagships is Calderdale's Dean Clough Industrial Park, where 180 firms now employ more than 1800 people in mills shut when Crossley Carpets closed in 1982. The inspiration of a private sector entrepreneur member of the Calderdale Partnership, Dean Clough is a living testimony to what can be done by public and private sector collaboration and a constant encouragement to further projects for economic and social regeneration at a time when Halifax seemed itself to be facing the same future as the carpet manufactory.

There are other ways of stimulating and encouraging the participants. A visit from a Royal personage provides very high profile status and is low-cost except in nervous energy. The interest of the Prince of Wales in the Calderdale partnership provides great stimulus. The simple manifestation of high-level interest by the sponsoring organisations create an aura of importance. The participants can see a tangible return on their investment in collaborative working.

## 8   RESOURCES

One of the most obvious ways to influence the behaviour of another agency is to give it money to accomplish objectives the Council pre-ordains but cannot achieve itself. Usually, of course, partnership implies input of resources from all partners, in cash or kind:

In 1986 the Lothian Regional Council became concerned that there were no facilities for drug dependent women to keep their children with them when admitted to rehabilitation facilities. In such circumstances there is a high risk of the children being placed in care. An independent child care trust put forward a proposal for a special unit which would accept women and their children. Edinburgh District Council released a block of flats to cater for a maximum of six parents and twelve children. The project started in April 1988 and is funded by the Department of Health, the Regional Council and the Lothian Health Board. Thus five agencies were persuaded to divert resources to the project by the Lothian Regional Council – which, if the scheme is successful, should save money by avoiding the need to take children into care.

Local authorities have proved particularly successful in chasing sources of funds – whether from the Training Agency, the European Social Fund, the European Regional Development Fund, Urban Programme or joint funding from the Health Service. Money is, though, not always the key. Schemes jointly financed by health authority and local authority have aroused increasing suspicion by local authorities because of the health authority contribution taper (currently over thirteen years). A scheme whereby a local authority gradually picks up the bill, until at the end of the day the scheme is entirely local authority funded, creates a reluctance to mortgage the financial future in such a way. Not only do some local authorities decline to participate in new joint finance schemes, but in some cases local authorities are abandoning existing schemes.

Certainly early joint ventures seemed to spring largely from the fertile minds of local authority social services departments rather than from the product of joint planning processes. They were often accepted by health authorities anxious to restrict the amounts of unspent monies to be carried forward at the year end. Health authorities came in some cases to believe that the joint finance schemes largely supported services which social services departments would have developed in any case. A national survey of health authorities conducted in 1982 found only 14 % reporting that joint finance had enabled them to influence social services departments' priorities. A follow-up survey in 1984 showed an increasing share of joint finance being taken up by health authorities – suggesting that instead of prompting collaborative activity it was serving as a reserve of extra cash for the health authorities.

In some cases the injection of finance may be unnecessary to achieve the aims of the Council. Sheltered housing, for example, is an area where County Councils can and often do pay a per unit grant to District Councils in respect of the sheltered housing units the latter provide. The result of the grant, explicitly or implicitly, is that the Area Social Services Directors have the opportunity to assess prospective tenants and make a priority nomination. However, in an increasing number of counties the grants have been withdrawn. It might be expected that the result would be a withdrawal by the District Council of the County Council's explicit or implicit right of assessment. This does not seem to result in practice, presumably because the

District Councils value the skills of the County's social services staff when making the assessments. In other words the input of the resource of professional expertise was adequate to secure the County Council's policies without the need for financial support.

If money becomes the lynchpin of the relationship, then joint working towards a common strategy often disappears. Too often existing plans are repackaged to suit the criteria of the funding agency. How many, for example, would argue that European finance has prompted any change in local authorities' provision? There is, however, the obverse danger: distortion of priorities in order to secure finance. Joint funding between health service and local authority for care in the community is an example. Bids for cash are judged against mechanical rules in relation to the specific project criteria. Such rigidity militates against systematic planning for the overall needs of a particular client group. Eagerness to acquire resources displaces commitment to overall objectives.

Such caveats are not to dispute that resources may be the key to influence on a partner. The willingness to divert them to the project may be an essential precondition of success. But it may be more effective to retain control of the resources in the hands of the Council rather than part with them to an organisation which could subvert or sub-optimise them. More subtle changes of resources may be more effective: e.g. the secondment of staff who would nevertheless retain a commitment to the values of their employer.

In some cases a partnership can include the extraction of resources by the local authority from the private sector for a socially desirable end. The private sector partner then assumes an interest in the success of the venture which might not arise had cash not been involved. An example is the Westminster sponsored litter bin project. Once a sponsor has paid for a litter bin outside the firm's premises then there is a chance of greater vigilance in ensuring that the bins are used.

Often a substantial motivator for a local authority in entering into a partnership is the inability of the local authority to finance the project internally and the need to obtain private sector finance. Such arrangements are particularly common in the housing field, where the partnership is cemented by transferring to the partner either development land or housing due for refurbishment. Where long-term schemes are launched with this as a main objective it is clearly in the interests of the local authority, as well as the partner, to ensure that the scheme is soundly based financially, with continued financial inducements for the private sector partners. Failure to observe this obvious precaution may cause the local authority to pick up an unexpected share of the ultimate bill:

> The Stockbridge Village Trust, launched with such acclamation in 1982 to regenerate a run-down area by refurbishment, development and a new social mix, had within three years hit a major financial crisis. Building costs had increased sharply. Existing residents could not afford to buy the refurbished housing. Few takers were found for the housing built for sale: instead of the 1110 target home owners there were just 56. The social mix had hardly changed. Crime and vandalism continued. Department of the Environment consultants concluded that the scheme had been launched without a proper financial assessment of its viability by the

private sector. Further central and local government funds had to be produced to enable the scheme to continue precariously. There seems likely to be a long-term gap between revenue from rents and running costs.

## 9  THE RIGHT SKILLS

If a partnership is to work then local authorities must employ staff with the requisite skills. For many years the conventional wisdom has been that local authorities appoint their Chief Officers on the basis of their professional abilities rather than upon the managerial skills which they will need in running a large bureaucracy. Much time and effort has been spent in training professionals to become managers. The generalist has made little impact in local authority service departments because of their professional bias.

If local authorities are to diminish as direct providers of services and become enablers and regulators then different skills will be needed. The Griffiths report (1988) envisages a Director of Social Services who will not head a large bureaucracy making direct provision but who will put together a package of provision from a variety of sources. Key skills will be a capacity for strategic thought and planning; a strong political awareness – including an awareness of the internal culture and politics of other agencies; strong inter-personal skills; and the networking skills to link together the right people on the right problems. The Director of Social Services would become an entrepreneur.

Michael Clarke and John Stewart in their publication *Managing Tomorrow* (1988) canvassed a need for managers:

▽  who are able to take as broad and unfettered view as possible;
▽  who can manage contracts or operate within a contractual framework and who can adopt a marketing perspective;
▽  who are skilled in the business of influencing, of understanding organisational and people development, and of coping with paradox and uncertainty;
▽  who are entrepreneurial in the sense of constantly looking for opportunities to innovate and find new ways of working to improve the effectiveness of the organisation;
▽  and who recognise that local government requires political direction and needs to manage with political sensitivity and awareness.

Such needs have an implication not only on the criteria against which selection panels judge candidates for Chief Officer appointments; they have an impact on the management development policies of the local authority as a whole. Such programmes must in future seek to develop marketing and entre-preneurial skills with specific regard to inter-organisational relationships.

## 10  SHARED POWER

A local authority which wishes to play Svengali to a partner's Trilby is in for a disappointment. In the words of the Home Office Working Group on Juvenile Crime (1987):

Meaningful co-operation depends on agencies being willing to share status and power. Co-operation begins with sharing concern about a problem which is common to all agencies and an acknowledgement that individual action by single agencies cannot resolve the problem. Planning of joint action will produce shared values which should overcome traditional reservations about sharing information and responsibility for activities which may not be a direct concern of the individual agency. Working together on common aims usually produces enthusiasm for participation towards the results which the agencies wish to achieve. In the right atmosphere traditional reservations about operational responsibilities and power rapidly disappear.

The last two sentences reflect a somewhat bland optimism. Councillors are jealous of their powers – especially in relation to agencies whose functions should, they suspect, be theirs. Even more damaging to inter-agency power sharing is the insularity of professional training. The 'professional' answer is often seen by the professional as the 'only' approach. Professional stereotypes seem to some extent to be justified by research; and often professions with most professional contact are those with least psychological affinity – planners and engineers, social workers and doctors are examples. Turf battles between professionals are a problem. Even more of a problem may be the reluctance of a professional to enter on the turf of another: witness the lack of challenge to professional discretion in the Cleveland child abuse cases. Most major disasters of which I have personal knowledge result from the failure to trespass on the turf of another professional and to ask key questions which might be thought to challenge professional status.

Joint training, preferably involving a strong social contact, is the key to overcoming these battles. Joint work on the problems of a client group and the relevant contributions of the different agencies can overcome professional rivalries, especially where a commitment to the needs of the client group is a strong motivation. Involvement by those concerned in the joint planning of a strategy is more likely to overcome professional problems than the handing down from on high of a strategy for implementation. Effective joint management systems must complement the joint planning process.

A formal system for joint planning of the project is very desirable. If one partner is seen to be in charge and the others performing merely an advisory role, the enthusiasm of the latter will rapidly diminish. Delegated management responsibility to a jointly managed initiative can be vital in ensuring its success. Budget provision for the mentally handicapped in Westminster is made by the City Council, the three Health Authorities and the voluntary sector. It is given to a joint committee of all three sectors with discretion as to its spending. Of course the mentally handicapped have a finite and known need, unlike the needs of the mentally ill. Nevertheless the agencies plan to experiment with shared budgets in this field too. Apart from creating commitment through joint ownership, the pooling of budgets ensures that organisational boundaries do not distort artificially the use of resources.

The West Yorkshire Archives Service was a bone of contention between the County Council and the Metropolitan Districts for almost a decade. The West Riding County Council prided itself as being the only County which had not appointed a County Archivist. The lack was deeply felt in the world of Yorkshire academe. Academics took advantage of the creation of the new West Yorkshire Metropolitan County Council in 1973 to extract pledges of commitment to an archive service. They were duly implemented: the new County Archives Service was created under distinguished leadership and to a high professional standard. The Metropolitan District Councils retaliated. Although their predecessor authorities had employed only one archivist between them (in Leeds), the establishment of the County Archives Services was sufficient to inspire a passionate pride in local records. In an area of activity hitherto thought remote from *Sturm und Drang*, violent passions erupted. Unseemly scenes took place as archivists canvassed confused donors with the respective virtues of their services. The Department of the Environment, called to adjudicate, held formal hearings with assessors from the Public Record Office and the Historical Manuscripts Commission. Eventually a spirit of compromise was precariously reached. A joint administration was agreed in an atmosphere of the utmost suspicion. The arrangement worked perfectly. Absorbed in professional matters, both the members on the Joint Archives Committee and the archivists themselves found it simple to work happily together – especially as the arrangement was lubricated by finance from the County Council. Ironically the joint arrangements were concluded as the knell for the County Council sounded. The joint arrangements survived the expiry of the County Council quite comfortably.

The sharing of power procured the result all actors sought. Eventually the primacy of the service rose above the turf battles of county and district.

There is some qualification to this concept of sharing of power: such projects usually need a driving actor, someone charged with accomplishing the end. If it is no one's responsibility to drive things forward, progress becomes no one's responsibility and affairs drift. In matters of extreme sensitivity an outsider can be appointed as a neutral to fulfil this role:

Southwark Council convened a conference on drug abuse in 1984 as a first step towards concerted action to tackle the problem. The conference set up a working party and the Council created a post of Drug Abuse Officer to provide support to the working party. Since many local services were involved, it was thought important that no one agency or group should be, or be seen to be, in control. For this reason an independent chairman – the co-ordinator of the standing conference on drug abuse – was invited to take the chair.

## 11  POOLING OF DATA

There is a great lack of shared data between statutory agencies. Often the data collected by one agency can greatly illuminate the decision taking of another. The swapping of data can inspire another agency to share a problem. Through the data the importance of the problem becomes recognised. There are difficulties in the pooling of data:

▽  The information may be thought to be confidential.
▽  Lack of mechanisms to permit pooling.
▽  Differences in operational boundaries.
▽  Inability to break information down to a convenient format.
▽  Suspicion between agencies as to the way in which the information will be used.

All these objections can, with patience, be overcome. Computerised data collection can form a basis for disaggregation to boundaries which can suit a multiplicity of agencies. Confidentiality can nearly always be preserved by the removal of means of identification from the data. Local authorities, for example, have no interest in knowing the identity of criminals, provided that data on crime is available to them in a sufficiently disaggregated form to help their own decision taking. Provision of such data can certainly play a major part in inspiring a local authority to take a much more dynamic approach to crime prevention.

Data taken for granted by one partner may sometimes come as a thunderbolt to another and can motivate a commitment to the solution of the relevant problem.

## 12   ONE BOSS

If partnership involves joint working by the staff of different agencies in one location it will smooth the path greatly if all the staff have one employer and similar conditions of service. Without this problems will constantly arise and differences be magnified:

> In West Cumbria a scheme for mentally handicapped people was run by a board of trustees. The staff employed had a choice of being employed by the Health Authority or the Social Services Department. The agency chosen would determine the conditions of service and salary scales of those involved. One member from each of four organisations (Health Authority, Local Authority, Local MIND organisations) was on the board of trustees. The intention is that the trustees would ultimately have sole control of all housing for mentally handicapped people in the community, staff training and day care.

> Contrast a day care centre where control is shared similarly between Borough Council, Health Authority and Education Authority. The governing body includes members from all three. But all three maintain staff in the centre, each with their own conditions of service. Each has a functional head answerable to the parent authority. Although the centre provides a very valued service, its full potential cannot be realised because of the split responsibilities and the problems in resolving day-to-day issues between staff with different conditions of service – dramatically epitomised by the differences between those on teaching conditions of service and those on social services conditions of service.

Such problems can sometimes be sorted out by bringing in a further party, particularly a voluntary agency, who can employ the staff from the start; avoid demarcation disputes; provide a flexible employment package; and unified management.

## Conclusion

When seeking partnership with an outside agency, concentrate on copying parallel successes. Do not look for what went wrong elsewhere: there are too many different ways of getting things wrong. Copy success.

Above all if it is principally the Council's problem, do not expect the external agency to adjust. The Council must adjust. In some cases the Council may offer a *quid pro quo* to the other agency. But in all cases clarity of aim and shared values are essential to the success of partnership.

Money may be essential to make a partnership work; but if you have a link to an uncommitted partner the injection of resources may well be counter-productive.

Find effective ways of procuring involvement of middle management. Ensure that there is a driving force to the partnership. Be prepared to share power if that seems the best way to achieve overall success.

## Using this chapter

▲ *What partnerships has your authority established? Have you addressed problems which your authority cannot solve without external participation? If not, why not?*

▲ *Have you recognised the problems which partnerships can face? What steps have you taken to overcome them? Do your decentralised staff have enough autonomy to achieve local partnerships?*

▲ *Have you agreed precise aims with your partner? Have you limited initial objectives to what is attainable? (1)*

▲ *What steps have you taken to achieve co-terminosity? Are you prepared to organise the local authority to meet a partner's geographical needs? (2)*

▲ *Is achievement through partnership a key task for your senior management? (3)*

▲ *Is co-option to a Council Committee or project group likely to help partnership? (4)*

▲ *Is your middle management involved in and committed to partnership arrangements? What machinery can you create to secure their participation? (5)*

▲ *Is formal machinery necessary for partnership? Have you created it? (6)*

▲ *Have you taken positive steps to encourage participants in a partnership by ensuring an early success or high-profile recognition? (7)*

▲ *Is your Council prepared to commit resources to the partnership? Are you able to recognise the financial needs of the partner? Is a money injection a genuine and necessary contribution to success – or could it distort the scheme's objectives? (8)*

▲ *Do your managers have the right skills? Are they good at influencing external agencies, creating packages and conceptualising a strategic dimension which exceeds the local authority's powers? (9)*

▲ *Is your Council prepared to share power and credit with an external partner? What steps have you taken to enable protagonists to understand cultures and share objectives? (10)*

▲ *Are you able to share data with your authority's partners? Do you receive from them the data you require in a form in which you can use it? Have you taken steps to adjust your data to meet the needs of the partnership? (11)*

▲ *In project-orientated partnerships, is one boss in charge? (12)*

# 6 Part ownership: joint boards and joint committees

**Key points**

▲ *Local government has had a long but fairly unhappy history of partnership through joint arrangement*
▲ *The characteristics of joint authorities – representational, strategic and administrative – are different*
▲ *The success of joint working can be improved if key factors are taken into account at the outset – and particularly if the local authority has a right to specify and pay for the level of service it requires*
▲ *A local authority must have a strategy towards joint bodies if it is to have a chance of influencing them*
▲ *Means of influence include effective representation, persuasion, procurement of allies, the application or withdrawal of money, the bringing to bear of external influence or the introduction or threat of constitutional change*

## Characteristics

Part ownership is distinguished in the minds of local government practitioners from partnership. Partnership implies a voluntary joining together where at all stages the consent of the partners is required not only to expenditure but also to actions. Part ownership has a number of characteristics:

▽ It is a permanent or semi-permanent association of a formal character.
▽ It is often, though not always, formed under compulsion, threat of compulsion or a compelling need to work together in the face of external demands.
▽ Withdrawal of the parties is often either impossible or inhibited by constitutional safeguards, e.g. compensation payments.
▽ Local authorities comprise all or most of the part owners.
▽ There are usually several part owners.

As an effective shareholder through part ownership, a local authority in theory has an element of control. Like the powers of the shareholder in a public company, that reality can often be illusory. A joint body can often have either legal or *de facto* powers to bind its constituent members. The inhibitions on withdrawal may operate to override the wishes of the constituent local authorities. Often the large number of protagonists makes the influence of any one local authority part owner small.

## Constitutional types

### JOINT BOARDS

A joint board is a corporate body: it can employ staff, litigate in its own name and hold land. Most importantly it can demand money from its constituent local authorities by precept, without needing their consent. It can also borrow money and may have an independent capital allocation from the Government. It is created by Act of Parliament, Statutory Regulation or Ministerial Order. Its constituent councils are specified in the legislative provision or order. Their representatives hold office according to the legislative provision. In some cases they can be recalled at will. In others they are appointed for a specified term. For some joint boards, representatives have to be appointed in accordance with the political balance of the nominating local authority.

### JOINT COMMITTEES

Joint committees are normally set up under Section 102 of the Local Government Act 1972. They are not corporate bodies, that is they cannot employ staff, hold land or litigate in their own name. In these capacities they must use one or more of their constituent members. Most crucially, they cannot raise money from constituent councils except by the agreement of those councils. Each council has, in effect, a right of veto which may lead to the withdrawal of that council from the joint committee unless a compromise is reached. Often joint committees are based on a formal agreement which inhibits such rights by applying a period of notice or by requiring compensation to be paid. Joint committees can be dissolved by agreement among their constituent councils. The need for joint committees to secure the agreement of constituent councils acts as an inhibitor on their spending: comparison of national parks authorities, where some are joint boards and others joint committees, suggests that joint boards are inclined to spend more than joint committees.

### HYBRIDS

There are variations in the concept of joint committees at both ends of the spectrum. Statute may impose a particular regime on a joint committee. Thus the London Boroughs Joint Grants Committee, created under Section 48 of the Local Government Act 1985, requires expenditure decisions to be made by two-thirds of the constituent councils. The remaining third may be bound by the majority view. However the decisions on spending are taken by the councils themselves, not by the joint committee. At the other end of the spectrum joint arrangements may be based on a loose association, with a lead borough taking all relevant decisions, consulting the part owner local authorities only on changes or developments. In effect those authorities buy services on a more or less structured basis from the lead borough.

## Functional types

### REPRESENTATIONAL

Local authorities have found it desirable to join together in associations to ensure that their interests are represented – whether to Government or to other agencies. Examples are the national associations of local authorities, together with regional groupings like the London Boroughs Association and the Association of London Authorities. The constitutions of the associations govern the representation of the constituent councils, often on a geographical basis. They are politically controlled (or hung) and their attitudes stem from the policies of the majority party. Initiatives stem from the controlling group. This can cause tension particularly on representation, where the geographical basis may exclude permanently some districts, a problem which is currently being addressed by the associations. For the most part councils under the control of a party in a minority on the association see advantages in, and continue their membership of, the association, though significant policy differences have prompted the resignation of one or two councils and the schism between the London Boroughs Association and Association of London Authorities. The Associations (with the exception of the one party Association of London Authorities) attempt a bi-partisan stance on issues like representation, and the constitution of the London Boroughs Association in particular insists that minority views are represented. The continuance of the associations depends upon the perception of member authorites that it is in their interests to belong.

Councils in particular localities also form associations, principally with a view to advocacy on behalf of their region, though they might also assume a strategic planning role. Bodies such as tourist boards and development associations bestride the functions of representation and administration. They market their regions to secure economic benefits but also administer services. Central Government is a major funder of these organisations and makes its funding conditional upon the adoption of certain structures and policies.

### STRATEGIC

Strategic joint bodies address issues of planning, policy making and resourcing. They were common before the reorganisations of local government and still survive in organisations such as SERPLAN. Their voluntary nature proves a great inhibitor: there is a necessity to carry with them all or at least all significant member authorities. This leads to the adoption of policies which arrive at the lowest common denominator or (in the case of bids for resources) the highest common factor. Understandably this tends to undermine their credibility. The statutory variant is the London Planning Advisory Committee, with the remit to give planning advice to the Secretary of State on a strategy for Greater London. Arising out of the abolition of the Greater London Council, its existence was hastily announced in the House of Lords by a Government intent to demonstrate that a pan-London planning capability would survive.

## ADMINISTRATIVE

Administrative joint bodies have been created by local authorities, voluntarily or under threat, for a variety of purposes. They have also been created by Government. One of the most common is an *ad hoc* joining for the purpose of a study or a piece of research. Joint bodies carry out a variety of administrative tasks ranging from the administration of archives to purchasing operations. History records the existence of a Joint Steam Roller Committee and a Joint Hearse Committee. They thrived in the days before reorganisation, when small authorities could not justify undertaking a function on their own. They have recently re-multiplied with the abolition of the Metropolitan County Councils and the Greater London Council, whose demise spawned a large number of joint bodies administering services from ecology to welfare rights. Often only a minority of boroughs were prepared to participate. Membership is compulsory for Government created joint bodies for example police, fire, waste regulation, the Lea Valley Regional Park.

## Attitudes

Historically joint bodies have not enjoyed unqualified success. Many have been disbanded as soon as the constituent local authorities could conveniently form an independent service, e.g. London Trading Standards Joint Committees. Local authorities still dislike joint bodies. As single purpose operations, they do not take account of competing demands on resources and prioritise their own services with which they are naturally preoccupied. They have been unsuccessful in involving constituent councils in their decision taking. They have tended to be officer dominated, particularly by the profession concerned. The absence of experienced officers with a general brief has tended to give *carte blanche* to the professionals. Local authority suspicions are particularly strong in the case of joint boards, which constrain constituent councils to financial commitments through a precept. At a time of financial retrenchment, sharp increases by a joint board free from direct accountability to the electorate can infuriate a constituent council. The joint bodies prize autonomy and are naturally anxious to expand their resources. Both ambitions grate on constituent local authorities. The distaste for joint committees is strongly demonstrated by the inner London boroughs who, in planning for their 1990 takeover of education from the Inner London Education Authority (a joint board by constitution), have eschewed joint bodies wherever possible. The boroughs have been content to leave services with a single borough, with the right to others to buy in and, perhaps, share proceeds in the event of disposal of any assets transferred to the lead borough.

Joint bodies have normally been most successful in the following circumstances:

▽   Where the constituents are of equal status; the involvement of another tier of local government has often led to bitter turf battles.
▽   When the joint arrangements are entered into voluntarily and without compulsion or threat, i.e. where the constituent councils see a mutual advantage in joining.

▽   Where the joint arrangements provide a service significantly cheaper than can be provided by the local authority single-handedly, e.g. in purchasing.
▽   Where joint action takes place mostly through officer mechanism and not through member agreement.
▽   Where policy making, planning or resourcing are excluded.
▽   Where the number of protagonists is limited.

The more constituents, then the more chance there is of a veto being used. On the other hand the participation of only two part-owning local authorities can lead to a stalemate, e.g. the block on the second runway at Manchester airport where the Greater Manchester Council and the Manchester City Council disagreed. A small number may also lead to the spectacle of two part owners of an operation being opposed by the third, e.g. the objection of Leeds City Council to the runway extension at Leeds/Bradford Airport, supported by the West Yorkshire Metropolitan County Council and the Bradford City Council.

## The need for a strategy

In some cases the activities of a joint body concern a part owning local authority little, causing no financial problems and creating little vexation. So it is possible for a member of a purchasing consortium to use the consortium only where it is cost effective so to do. The need for active consideration of its plans may arise only when, for example, there is a need for capital expenditure calling for a contribution from constituent councils. In the case of other joint bodies the sole concern of a constituent local authority may be to minimise its spending. Its services may be of little interest to a local authority which has been forced to accept them.

Joint bodies delivering administrative services often have a great impact upon the constituent council. The extent to which the council will wish to influence it will depend upon the importance attached to the services provided by the joint body in the constituent council's area. Thus the receiving boroughs have a strong interest in creating and influencing joint action by the all-London Borough committee on homelessness, seeking a code of practice which would rationalise and limit the demand on their services.

A council may seek to influence a joint fire board in the location of a new fire station. Certainly local councils wish to influence joint bodies for passenger transport in the services they are prepared to subsidise in that council's area.

Even more important is the ability of a part owning authority to influence a strategic joint body. In the case of voluntary associations, the authority will seek to divert effort or resources into its own area. The local authority associations can be encouraged and exhorted to press for Government policies which will suit the member council. Even more importantly the associations will be asked to press for revenue support grant formulae which will be of benefit. In the case of joint bodies imposed upon part owning councils by compulsion, the councils may often seek to limit the interference of those bodies in the running of the council's own affairs, so as to secure maximum freedom from external influence. The councils cannot simply rely on part ownership to secure compliance with their wishes by a joint body whose members are often more dedicated to the joint body than to the nominating council. The leverage which they are able to exert is often less than that which they can exert through partnership or partial control. The local authority must be clear in its mind as to the areas where it wishes to influence a joint body and exert itself accordingly. A mini-strategy is required for each, forming part of the authority's vision for its own area.

If the activities of a joint body are to be influenced then they must be monitored. There must be a capacity to understand the technical issues discussed, a knowledge of the cycle of decision taking of the body, and its pre-occupations. Intervention must be timely.

## Means of influence

### 1  REPRESENTATION

The most obvious means of influence is through the constituent council's representative or representatives on the joint body. However in law the representative is a nominee, not a delegate. That is to say he or she is free to exercise his or her own judgment, priorities and prejudices. The representative is not bound by the wishes of the nominating local authority, as would be a delegate. It is a common complaint of local authorities that representatives assume the values of the joint body and not those of the constituent council.

It is often difficult for a council to choose a satisfactory representative. The Leader of the Council will usually wish to keep his most able members in key committee chairs in his own authority. A nomination to an outside body is rarely seen as greatly desirable. Control of a joint body may be within the patronage of leaders, but their room for manoeuvre is limited. Regional joint bodies often meet during the day, consume much time and are effectively out of bounds to working members or those already shouldering the burdens of committee chairs. Control of joint bodies is often shared between a gerontocracy and a gynaecocracy. Where less influential members are nominated to it, it is not surprising that they 'go native', since the joint body represents their own position of authority and power base. It is the post which offers them the greatest prestige and influence.

The representative on a joint body faces a formidable task in persuasion. He is removed from his usual colleagues, on whom he can count for support. He is faced with a body of professional expertise which his own council cannot match. He has no 'independent' officers from the Chief Executive's or Treasurer's Department on whom he can lean for moral support. The chairman of the joint board is often in cahoots with its chief officer. His party group may well be much more loosely organised than that of a council. Party solidarity may be less sure and be difficult to win.

Despite these disadvantages a council's representative on a joint board is the obvious first point of attack if its policies or activities are to be influenced. If it is a body whose activities are important to a nominating council, then the quality of the representative is vital. Even more important is the time that the representative can spare. It is also necessary that officers should track the joint board in order to brief the representative; he cannot influence without positive and expert briefing. If the authority itself has insufficient expertise and the activities of the joint board are important enough, then such expertise must be bought. It is, for example, quite simple to find competent officers who would be willing to offer part time consultancy advice and would undertake the task of analysing and commenting on a joint body's papers. Above all, the nominating council must be clear on the points of inter-action which it seeks to influence.

There remains always a sanction in the hands of the constituent council – at least in the case of the joint committees (and some joint boards). This is to recall the representative and replace him by one who is more prepared or more able to represent the council's view. If membership of the outside body is seen as desirable, then even the threat of removal may be sufficient. In at least some cases the law may prevent recall before the end of the normal term of appointment. The threat may have to be of a deferred removal.

## 2   PERSUASION

Any organisation is open to persuasion. At its most straightforward, an advocacy case can be made, relying upon marshalled facts and data. If the authority can show that the joint board under-provides in its area then it can expect a responsive hearing. It will be easier to persuade a joint body to enlarge its service rather than to restrict it elsewhere: joint bodies are normally sympathetic to the idea of enlarging their empires.

On the same line of thought, a *quid pro quo* can be given in exchange: support to enlarge activities elsewhere, if a modification is made to a service. A fuss can be made. No joint body likes trouble, though its lack of direct accountability makes it more immune from popular pressures than a local authority. Nevertheless a climate of popular opinion and constant pressure – with the right case – can influence its behaviour.

## 3   ALLIES

If a constituent council seeks to procure from a joint board a benefit solely for itself then it will have an uphill task, unless it can demonstrate clearly that it suffers unreasonably from the service it receives. It is more likely to be successful if a case can be made which procures benefits for others. Allies can be sought and identified. Often such alliances may be within political parties but equally as often may be geographically based.

It is unlikely that the constituent council is alone in holding a certain view. It is important to identify other authorities with like interests and, through contact with them, persuade their representatives to support the case. It may be possible to achieve alliances between officers of the joint board and officers of the local authority: such will be extremely potent in achieving results.

In some cases it may be perceived that the willingness of the joint board to change is caused by pressure on its chairman. Where there are powers of recall, it is possible for a grouping of boroughs including the chairman's nominating authority to threaten to remove him; or even to do so if he or she proves recalcitrant. Such a sharp shock can be very effective in creating a change of direction.

The skills of alliance building are natural to politicians, but they take time and effort. It is necessary to persuade those involved that the end result is worth the trouble. The geographical separation of the parties and the difference of interests makes alliance building in such bodies particularly time consuming. However a lunch organised by the activist constituent council can often be a cost effective way of creating a move for change.

## 4  MONEY – ITS SUPPLY OR DENIAL

The easiest way of influencing a joint board to a certain course of action is to undertake to bear the costs directly. Thus the Greater Manchester Council achieved quick success through joint committees in improving the environment of its river valleys by the simple expedient of bearing the expense itself. The West Yorkshire Metropolitan County Council was able to secure improvements to the archive service similarly. Such expedients are not so easy for part owners from the same tier of government. Nevertheless it may be open to them to agree to pay more for a specified service in their own borough. Most of the historic objections to joint committees and joint boards would be overcome if constituent councils could specify the service which they wished to receive, in much the same way as they do in relation to contracted out services.

This may not be so easy in the case of joint boards as at present constituted. Often the local authority may have no power to bear the expense of a service transferred out of its immediate control. Indeed the more usual concern with joint boards is to find means of limiting their expenditure. Normally there will be a statutory consultation process – or at worst an informal consultation process. The process can be used to extract information from a joint body, to analyse its spending and to press for improvements in value for money or cuts in services. It may be open to the joint board to decline such suggestions, but sustained pressure over a period of time will not normally bear some, even if limited, fruit. More ways of influencing expenditure may be tried. A constituent council might, for example, offer to bear the costs of a consultancy study into the services in its area. If such a study is commissioned by the joint board (even if financed by a constituent council) the joint board may find it difficult to shrug off conclusions. Clearly a constituent council would have to be sure of its ground or at least optimistic before embarking on such an enterprise.

More direct action is possible in the case of joint committees. The constituent council can veto the expenditure. Some joint bodies have special expenditure accounts for fighting funds or building acquisition. The local authority can refuse to contribute. It can even threaten total withdrawal, with a consequent effect upon the contributions of other constituent councils. Such action may sour relationships unless there are known to be substantial allies. It will nevertheless force a compromise to be reached. In the case of the hybrid London Boroughs Grants Committee, a long running impasse in 1987 forced the Secretary of State to threaten to impose a maximum figure for the total grant giving. All three political parties accepted the compromise, one suspects with some relief, since voluntary organisations dependent upon funding were starting to issue redundancy notices to staff. Because of financial commitments out of their control, London boroughs have been prepared to withdraw from the Taxicard Scheme inherited from the GLC and substitute their own financially controlled scheme. Vetos and withdrawals of this sort call for a strong nerve and political backing. They should not be embarked upon without both, but given them are incontrovertibly effective.

## 5   EXTERNAL INFLUENCE

It is worth considering what external influence can be brought to bear on a joint body. The intervention of the Secretary of State in the London Boroughs Joint Grants Scheme is an example. The climate of public opinion may be effective if it is wound up as part of a sustained campaign. The attitude of the London Docklands Development Corporation to community involvement seems to be significantly affected by the climate of opinion created by Docklands boroughs resentful of the inability of local communities to share in the benefits of development. As a result a climate of partnership is being created where none existed before. Ministers often retain some powers in relation to joint boards: control of expenditure, establishment and the like. Advocacy to Government, if successful, can bring results. In the case of a body such as the London Planning Advisory Committee, the ultimate decision on its advice rests with the Secretary of State who will obviously receive advocacy from individual boroughs in relation to his reaction to the LPAC strategy. Thus boroughs discontented with LPAC's plans have a second bite of the cherry. The activities of a joint body can be influenced by systematic lobbying and the distribution of public information.

More precise targeting can take place. A local authority has access to and to some extent can influence pressure groups in its own areas. It can, for example, direct voluntary organisations towards applying for support from a joint grants scheme, thus maximising the scheme's potential contribution to its own area and indirectly minimising the call on its own financial resources. Bodies of traders can be incited to press for greater activity in a particular sector from a trading standards joint committee. Passenger consultative committees can be fed information on problems in the transport network so that they can be prompted to pressurise the supply bodies.

The constituent council retains legal powers which may be deployed to influence the joint body, e.g. in the fields of licensing, regulation and planning. The help of the local authority in data assembly could be vital. It is always possible, too, for a local authority to seek judicial review of the activities of a joint body in order to influence its decisions. Thus a constituent member of the London Boroughs Grants Scheme successfully sought the intervention of the courts on the way in which the joint scheme committee interpreted its constitutional remit to distribute funds to organisations covering more than one borough. And in the most famous case, the London Borough of Bromley successfully sought a reversal of the Greater London Council's decision on cheap fares. A major part of the borough's motivation was the absence of underground services in Bromley and the corresponding inability of their own residents to take full advantage of the GLC's scheme. Wrangles in the courts may seem unseemly but can often be effective if all else fails.

## 7   CONSTITUTIONAL CHANGE

The functioning of a body can be significantly affected by constitutional change. At its most basic a local authority can withdraw from the joint committee. It can seek partition of a joint board – as the West Midlands Boroughs unsuccessfully did for the West Midlands Police Joint Committee. Joint committees – and joint boards – can often be based on a lead borough. A change in the lead borough may have a significant effect upon the operation of the joint body. Officers of the lead borough develop a greater expertise in the functions of a joint body, become correspondingly influential and can be able to provide an informed counter-balance to the power of the chief officer. Such an ally can be invaluable if constituent councils wish to change the orientation of the joint body. The perceived significance of the lead borough in political terms can be seen in the choice by the London boroughs of Richmond as lead borough for the joint grants scheme. A 'neutral', i.e. Alliance-controlled actor was acceptable when Conservative and Labour candidates were not.

Other constitutional changes may have great significance. In London, for example, most joint bodies charge on the basis of population. A change may be constitutionally possible to, for example, the basis of use, or vice versa. Such a change has a great impact on the contributions made by constituent councils to a scheme such as the London Concessionary Fares Schemes. An alliance of benefiting boroughs imposed such a change on unwilling part owners. Translated into charging for the Lee Valley Regional Park, the balance of payments would shift heavily towards north London boroughs. Further constitutional changes can limit the discretion of joint committees by agreement between the constituent councils. The London Concessionary Fares Scheme, for example, has a universally disliked statutory reserve scheme. Its existence as fallback induces reluctant boroughs to continue membership of the existing scheme. Legally binding constitutions may be created which can, for example, call for a two-thirds majority on funding. Constitutions can lay restrictions on the activities of joint bodies which constituent councils feel unable to impose through vigilance year on year. Such changes will require the consent of all constituent councils but if the time is right that consent may be possible.

## Conclusion

Paradoxically joint bodies controlled by local authorities can give little opportunity for direct influence by the constituent local authorities. Joint boards can often be officer led and follow their own objectives which may not be consistent with those of the constituent councils. Joint committees may often be frustrated through the inability of constituent councils to agree. Because of these drawbacks local authorities have historically been less than enthusiastic about joint arrangements.

Representational joint bodies have been the most successful, having as their main objective advocacy for the constituent councils. Administrative joint bodies with little policy content have also been successful. Strategic or policy making joint bodies have been least effective.

Nevertheless there are various ways in which constituent councils can influence joint bodies, most of which are neglected. In particular there is the careful choice of representatives, fully briefed by the local authority, who can

be a major source of influence. For the future local authorities may increasingly
see joint bodies as working more like contractors, i.e. delivering services to the
specification of the constituent council, with payment being made according to
the level of service required and provided. This development may overcome
the historic distaste for joint arrangements.

## Using this chapter

▲ *Are all the joint bodies on which your council is represented necessary? Have
you reviewed their functions? Is it possible for the council to withdraw from
them?*

▲ *Which of the joint bodies deliver services which are key to the council's own
plans for its area? Do you have friendly relationships with the officers of these
bodies? Do you follow their activities closely? Are members of your staff
specifically briefed to track the key agencies in order that timely intervention
in their deliberations may be possible?*

▲ *Are your representatives on joint bodies chosen with regard to the importance
of the joint bodies' functions? Do they have enough clout? Are they fully briefed
on key issues? Has your council recalled a representative who is not adequately
representing the authority's point of view? More fundamentally, are candidates
for council elections able to spare the necessary time to devote to these bodies?
(1)*

▲ *Has your authority supplied expertise or data to a joint body with a view to
influencing its decisions? Has your council contemplated servicing a key joint
body in order to develop a knowledge of its workings? Have you volunteered
help to a joint body in its policy development? (2)*

▲ *Does your council have recognised allies among the participants in a joint
body? Have you taken steps to identify convergent interests so that joint action
by constituent councils can be taken? Is the chairman sympathetic to your
authority's needs? (3)*

▲ *Have you contemplated trying to influence a joint body by the injection of
resources, either in cash or in kind? (4)*

▲ *If a joint body is taking action inconsistent with your council's aims, have you
contemplated what could be done to influence it? Are its decisions strictly
constitutional? Have you contemplated judicial review as a means of changing
a decision? (5)*

▲ *In extremis has your council contemplated withdrawal from a joint body either
in principle or as a method of influencing its decisions? (6)*

▲ *Has your council contemplated seeking constitutional change to the joint body
in order to give a bigger stake in its decision taking? Is it possible to change
the basis of funding of the joint body so as to advantage your council? (7)*

# 7 Purchasing: the use of the market

## Key points

▲ *With the growing centralisation of purchasing, opportunities exist for local authorities to use their purchasing power as an instrument of policy despite government restrictions*

▲ *Some local authority practices have effectively removed the opportunity for local companies to compete*

▲ *By liaison with local manufacturers, product specifications and quantities may be revised to promote local manufacture and thus employment*

▲ *Purchasing policies can also influence the environment*

▲ *By using its purchasing power, a council can enhance the choice of its residents or make available cheaper goods*

## Recent developments

Local government buys substantial quantities of goods from the market place. In total its annual purchases amount to over £3 billion. Each local authority is a major procurement agency.

Many local authorities have come to realise the advantage that their purchasing power gives them in the market place. Unco-ordinated purchases by different departments are being replaced by central procurement arrangements. In many parts of the country councils have access to large purchasing agencies, sometimes run jointly like Yorkshire Purchasing, in other cases run by one authority, like Kent County Council, but used by a variety of others. In either case the union of demands gives substantial purchasing power which operates to provide an advantageous price.

The centralisation of purchasing has prompted local authorities to examine ways of using their purchasing power not only to secure value for money but also as a policy instrument. In some cases these have been stretched beyond what the Government deems to be appropriate to local authorities: for example the banning or promotion of the goods of certain countries like South Africa or Nicaragua. Contract compliance units have been set up in certain authorities to promote the authority's policies through purchasing. The Local Government Act 1988 now restricts the extent to which suppliers can be selected according to their records on, e.g. race relations and employment of local labour. Statute limits enquiries to certain questions in respect

D

of equal opportunities and health and safety and precludes the local authority from having regard to 'non-commercial' matters (see chapter 3).

## The influence of purchasing policies

The preoccupation of purchasing departments must be to secure continuity of supply, cheapness and quality. Apart from the use of purchasing as an instrument in securing equal opportunities, promoting safe working practices and influencing foreign policy, buying has been actively used by local authorities:

▽   to promote local firms;
▽   to use environmentally acceptable products;
▽   to help their residents or tenants.

## How to use purchasing for policy ends

### 1   A SPECIFICATION

Local authorities are becoming better at producing a specification which avoids the use of brand names. Originally done to cut costs and improve quality, a specification can be used as a means of creating local employment. The very specification may effectively rule out or promote a local product. It may be that with an acceptable change a locally manufactured product could be procured, thus stimulating local manufacturing industry and creating employment.

### 2   THE SIZE OF THE CONTRACT

There is an obvious view that more means cheaper, i.e. the bigger the quantities the greater the discounts that can be negotiated. This may not always be true; but if it is, the bulk required may effectively disqualify small local manufacturers from competing. If one of the council's policy objectives is to stimulate local employment, then quantities can be the subject of separate purchasing contracts in order to permit smaller local firms to compete. With the assurance of larger orders and proper price safeguards, it may be possible to guarantee a continuity and a size of order which could prompt local firms to expand and meet price criteria normally available only from larger contracts.

### 3   LIAISON WITH LOCAL FIRMS

Too often local firms are unaware of the purchasing capacity of their local authority. It is possible for the latter to take steps to remedy this. In conjunction with the local Chambers of Commerce, a local authority can list and circulate details of products it needs to acquire. In some cases local authorities have held exhibitions or other events to persuade local companies to compete with their products against goods procured elsewhere. It may be possible to change the product by discussion to one capable of local manufacture.

## 4 CONTRACTUAL PRACTICES

Some procedures of contract compliance units may have been counter-productive in dissuading local companies from competing. The rigour of some of the questionnaires may have deterred them. Such lengthy questionnaires are now largely outside the law; but local authorities can still ensure that their procurement practices are not such as to deter small companies by their complexity or their requirements for financial information, references, history of similar jobs completed and insurance limits.

## 5 THE ENVIRONMENT

In devising specifications, councils can have regard to the effect of the product on the local environment. For example they can specify the purchase of vehicles which use unleaded petrol. With a more global concern for the environment, they can restrict the use of chlorofluorocarbons in products they acquire on the assumption that these damage the ozone layer. Clauses such as this have been adopted by local authorities and, indeed, commended by the London Boroughs Association to its members. Some authorities try to avoid the use of tropical hardwoods where there is a suitable alternative in terms of costs and durability or where supplies can be obtained from a renewable source – though questions are raised as to whether hardwoods imported to this country do emanate from diminishing tropical rain forests.

## 6 BENEFITS TO RESIDENTS AND TENANTS

In some cases goods required by residents may be difficult to obtain and the local council may operate as a source of supply. It is not, for example, unusual for councils to make rock salt available to residents in winter, when other sources of supply may be difficult. The council may act as an agency to secure cost reductions for its tenants: the Glasgow Housing Department has, for example, obtained a cheap tariff from the Electricity Board. In some cases a local authority may prompt the development of a specific product which can then be made available for purchase by its residents. Sheffield developed a dehumidifier to reduce dampness in older housing. Its purchasing power secured a cheap price for purchasers as well as guaranteeing stability of production for a local manufacturer. Westminster has introduced a pioneering by-law requiring owners to clear up dog faeces from pavements. Convenient instruments to do this being difficult to obtain on the market, Westminster procured and made available for sale through its one-stop services points cardboard and plastic pooper-scoopers to give its residents a ready and hygienic means of compliance.

## Conclusion

Within the present law, it is still possible for the local authorities to use purchasing as an instrument of policy:

▽ to stimulate local manufacturers and contractors and provide employment;

$\nabla$   to protect the local environment;
$\nabla$   to provide choice and price benefits for residents and tenants.

**Using this chapter**

▲   *Have you considered the extent to which purchasing can be used by your council as an instrument of policy?*
▲   *Have you considered the extent to which local firms could act as your suppliers?*
▲   *Have you made sure that your demands do not rule them out of competing? (1–4)*
▲   *Can you improve the environment through your purchasing? (5)*
▲   *Can you intervene to prompt the market to improve services by suppliers – or reduce the cost – to your residents or tenants? (6)*

# 8 Support: the voluntary sector

**Key points**

▲ *There are substantial benefits from support to the voluntary sector*
▲ *The local authority must be clear in its aims in grant-giving*
▲ *There are mutual benefits in a contract with the supported agencies, in particular a clear statement of expected output and the conditions attached to the grant*
▲ *Participation in the management of the voluntary organisation may not be helpful, but its performance should always be monitored*
▲ *Be clear about the amount of support given by avoiding hidden subsidies and maintaining a central channel of support*
▲ *Rather than long-term staff support, consider aiding organisations by short-term secondments or consultancies*
▲ *The most effective help may be through providing premises, training, advice, help with fund-raising or making available specialised equipment.*

## Growth

Support by local government to the voluntary sector grew exponentially during the early 1980s. In 1981/2, for example, grants made to the voluntary sector by the GLC amounted to £4 million. By 1985/6 they had grown to over £60 million. The budget for the London Boroughs Joint Grants Scheme is still half that amount, despite much grant-making having been undertaken by individual boroughs. The City of Westminster, for example, in 1989/90 gave over £8 million to the voluntary sector. Among the reasons for this increase are:

▽ A growing perception of minority needs.
▽ A growing realisation that need cannot be met by statutory services alone.
▽ Urging by Government.

Of course not all support by local authorities goes to the voluntary sector. A local authority may decide to subsidise an unremunerative facility in its area by financing the owning company. More commonly a local authority may inject funds, directly or indirectly, into a commercial concern to persuade it to locate, expand or continue to operate in the Council's area. Such support does not confer any continuing influence on the company save in the rare case where an enterprise board might nominate a director to the firm's board as a condition of support. On the whole, though, the financial relationships between local authorities and commercial organisations or nationalised bodies take the form of contracting. The payments made to support public transport operations fall firmly into this category.

## The benefits of encouraging the voluntary sector

There are undoubted benefits in support channelled through the voluntary sector. Any local authority should, though, ask itself whether those benefits are real. Does a voluntary organisation make a genuine contribution to help need in the area? Or has it become an introverted oligarchy? Does it genuinely do good works? Or does it consist of those who ride on the authority's financial bandwagon? 'Voluntary' need not mean amateur. Certainly the substantial budgets of some voluntary organisations call for good, paid staff. There is an increasing realisation within the voluntary sector of the need for value for money and a professional approach.

The benefits of support to the voluntary sector include:

▽  Voluntary organisations are more able to use unpaid helpers than councils. Often these people are extremely dedicated, sometimes because of direct experience of the problems themselves. Parents with handicapped children, for example, will often take a much wider role in support to the handicapped. Such helpers augment manpower resources with great commitment and dedication. The retired can make a major contribution. Voluntary organisations can attract secondees from commerce and industry to bring a business approach or professional skills to their organisations. The local authority can often help by supporting a volunteer bureau or by using its contacts with the private sector.

▽  Voluntary organisations have greater flexibility than local authorities, particularly in the employment of staff. They can negotiate *ad hoc* and have much lower overheads than local authorities. They are a natural focus for trainees in community work on YTS schemes. They are able more easily to tailor working hours to employee requirements and can overcome some of the inflexibilities in local authority conditions of service. This last is especially important in establishments which employ staff of different disciplines and conditions of service – e.g. teachers, health workers and social workers. They can often offer great flexibility of service, with a capacity for innovation stemming from real closeness to the customer.

▽  Voluntary organisations are often able to procure resources themselves by fund raising which can augment the resources made available by the local authority. Often they may be arms of national bodies which are able to distribute funds to their local branches. Local commerce and industry find it easier, understandably, to contribute to voluntary organisations (often in kind through business links schemes) rather than to a local authority to whom they already make a large contribution through the rates. Often voluntary organisations are able to obtain cheap or free premises, usually on a temporary basis.

▽  Voluntary organisations provide a natural focus for participation and community involvement. Often their centres double up as a focus for community life, with interaction between donors and recipients of help – if indeed that distinction is meaningful. Voluntary organisations can make major contributions to campaigns such as waste recycling. Indeed the NCVO has created a Waste Watch project to promote community recycling schemes.

▽   Voluntary work provides therapy for those involved. Participants can gain status and esteem which they may lack through unemployment; or they can regain that which they held when they were in employment. The involvement of the disabled and minority groups may be particularly valuable and is an end in itself.

▽   In some cases it may be very desirable for an enterprise to function at arm's length from the local authority. This is particularly helpful in the arts, where local authorities have a long tradition of enabling rather than direct provision. Not only does a separate operation, constitutionally distinct from the local authority, have a better chance of attracting central funding, it also insulates the local authority from some of the controversies which occasionally surround the arts. It is politically embarrassing for a local authority to finance obscenity, blasphemy or nudity; it is equally embarrassing for them to impose censorship on arts organisations. The independence of the latter avoids the dilemma. Independent organisations, even pressure groups, may attract more support than an in-house operation. Thus Westminster was an agent in the formation of the National Amusement Arcade Action Group, which was effective in securing support from many local authorities for its campaign against amusement arcades.

▽   Voluntary organisations can provide pluralism in choice to consumers. Their provision can often be complementary to that of the local authority, e.g. nurseries, social work services. Often their community links enable them to provide a service more appropriately than the local authority.

## Drawbacks

There are also drawbacks to voluntary organisations. They can be unprofessional, unaccountable and undirected. The pouring of vast amounts of money into the hands of voluntary bodies, especially for capital projects, has a chequered history with some major disasters. Local authorities must be satisfied that groups have substantial direct expertise if they are to be entrusted with major areas of activity – and especially if they are in charge of open-ended and money-consuming capital projects. There is a loss of control over the service and the ultimate (and perhaps only) sanction of cutting grant can be unacceptably controversial. In such situations the buck tends to stop with the local authority, despite the independence of the voluntary organisation. But steps can be taken to overcome these problems.

## How to maximise the benefits from voluntary organisations

▽   The local authority must be clear in its aim in giving money to the voluntary organisation. Even if a general grant is given for good works, then the authority should be clear that those works are relevant to its overall strategy. They must meet some known need in the local authority's area.

▽ Grants may be given for general purposes without any clear statement of output. But where large sums are given and a substantial output expected, there is every benefit from the creation of a formal contract between voluntary body and local authority. This can bring certainty to the voluntary body, especially if the contract promises financial support over a period of time, e.g. three years. If substantial sums are entrusted to the voluntary body then it is only right that there should be a clear specification as to what services the organisation will provide in response. Thus the City of Westminster provides £1 million annually to Age Concern. The overwhelming majority of this goes towards the provision of day centres and associated transport for elderly people. The Council has an agreement with Age Concern specifying the services to be provided for an element of its funding. Such contracts may be unduly onerous on tiny organisations which could have neither the resources nor the ability to guarantee strict compliance with a measured output. Nor might it be appropriate if the voluntary sector is to retain innovatory capacity and flexibility, in any case at risk as voluntary organisations gear themselves up to a much larger scale of operations.

▽ The local authority may be able to impose both positive and negative conditions on the grants it makes. Even negative conditions may do something to promote the general objectives of the council, e.g. a prohibition on fly-posting. Other conditions may restrict certain activities by the voluntary organisations. These must be made explicit during the process of grant giving. A common condition is an undertaking by the voluntary body not to enter into political matters. There is a fine distinction between a local campaign on a particular issue, and a political campaign. Local authorities should be careful that such conditions do not prevent the voluntary body unduly from contributing to debate or serving its community of need. The local authority can ensure that its own funding is not used for campaigning. Positive conditions may secure certain positive actions by the voluntary organisations.

> The City of Westminster has launched a Residents' Card (Rescard) scheme which gives residents concessions at local establishments – cheap admission to exhibitions, theatres, the zoo, as well as to the Council's own leisure centres. Many commercial enterprises find it worthwhile to participate as a marketing tool. But the mainstay of the scheme is the participation by the arts organisations supported by the Council. These range from the English National Opera, English National Ballet, the Courtauld and Tate Galleries to the Institute for Contemporary Art and the Regent's Park Open Air Theatre. Apart from the actual concessions gained there is a great public relations gain in making residents aware of the benefits conferred upon them by the Council – particularly important during the era of the community charge. Participation in such a scheme may or may not be a condition of grant-giving – but is certainly a factor to be taken into account when grants are considered.

▽ The local authority can maximise its own public relations benefit by requiring voluntary organisations to acknowledge the council's support on, for example, its notices, programmes and letter heading. An arts organisation may organise special concessionary seats for Council nominees (e.g. the elderly and disabled) at greatly reduced prices. The City of Westminster organises (with co-sponsors) such weeks at the Royal Opera House and English National Opera – with substantial returns from public relations as well as the benefits enjoyed by those who could not otherwise afford such an experience.

▽   As part of the grant giving process, the local authority can monitor the provision by the organisation. It is common for assessors to be appointed to arts organisations. They are entitled to attend meetings and report back not only to the parent authority but also to the outside body. If a voluntary organisation is to be evaluated then this process must take place against clear goals established from the outset. In other words monitoring and evaluation depend upon a statement of what the council expects the voluntary organisation to provide. One of the most obvious checks is to see whether the provision by the organisation is in fact used and by how many people. A per client calculation of grant often produces surprising results – both ways. In some cases the grant per user can be disproportionately high; in other cases it can underline the paucity of local authority support. It is helpful to involve councillors in the assessment process. They often have local knowledge of organisations denied even to a central unit. Thus the City of Westminster circulates to its members a list of all the organisations (well over a hundred non-arts organisations) requesting grants. Councillors are given *pro formas* (and a direct telephone line) so that their comments can be taken into account during the grant-giving process.

▽   The local authority can participate in the management of the organisations, most commonly by appointing a representative to its management committee, but sometimes by putting an officer in the position of secretary. In some cases such participation can be very useful. But in most it is unsuccessful from the point of view of both the voluntary organisations and the council. The City of Westminster alone has the job of appointing nearly 400 representatives to outside bodies. The capacity of members of the Council to attend on a regular basis is small. Those members who do attend tend to be fired by missionary zeal for the organisation. They do fulfil the role of reporting back on activities to the Council but sometimes in such a partisan way as to discredit their findings with colleagues. Their utility as a council emissary to the organisation can be small.

## Means of support

### 1   MONEY

Local authorities often do not have a central knowledge of the money they distribute to voluntary organisations. Sometimes different arms of the authority can make separate contributions to the same organisation. No central understanding of its real financial position or need exists. If money is to be channelled to a voluntary organisation it is as well to use one channel.

E

Thus the City of Westminster has a Central Grants Unit through which all support to grant-aided organisations is made. The unit can act on recommendations of departments and their comments are put in front of members when decisions are taken. Such a central capacity concentrates expertise. It makes regular monitoring and contact with the organisations possible and systematic. Audited accounts can be demanded as a matter of routine and grants denied if they are not supplied. Financial expertise can be brought regularly to bear on the finances of organisations. In particular, hidden subsidies can be avoided. It is not infrequent for local authorities to provide cheap accommodation or support in kind. If local authorities are to have any idea of the true cost of support market rents and charges should be sought. The grant to the voluntary organisation can rise immediately to meet these costs. To do otherwise is not only to conceal the true cost of provision but also to give the voluntary organisation an incentive to distort its activities so as to maximise cheap provision. The authority's central unit can monitor achievement of the output specified by the local authority in its agreement with the voluntary body or as a condition of grant.

## 2   STAFF

It is common for local authorities to supply staff to voluntary organisations. Voluntary youth organisations can often be given the services of youth workers in terms of hours per week. There is a strong drawback to such provision. It is expensive to the local authority and distorts decision taking by the voluntary body. If that organisation has flexibility in the use of its resources it might be able to direct them more usefully. It might, for example, make more determined efforts to secure voluntary helpers if it could thereby redirect money spent on salaries. A hypothecated sum as part of the annual grant to cover the cost of staff would give the organisation the freedom to maximise benefits. If necessary, initial help can be given to the organisation in the setting up of costs for normal employment processes.

There are some exceptions. Local authorities have not copied the regular use by industry of secondment – either of employees who are surplus to requirements towards the end of their careers; or as training in the outside world for young managers on the way up. There can be great benefit both ways by the secondment of manpower. The organisation can get the benefit of expertise it could not normally afford. The authority would find a useful avenue of deployment for its staff as well as a chance of influencing the direction of the organisation. From time to time a quick consultancy by local authority staff or a secondee can make an enormous impact on an organisation which does not have the expertise or resources to examine itself. It may even change the relationship between the organisation and the Council:

> A charitable trust ran almshouses for the elderly. The council appointed two representatives to its committee of management. Neither were members of the council, but were elderly supporters of the majority party on the council. Both brought back damning reports of the incompetence and aggression of management. The home was not in the Council's area and authority staff had no inside knowledge. One or two visits did not confirm the reports. The council procured the free services of a consultant

who totally exonerated the management, save for one or two minor failings. The Council's representatives, though well intentioned, were mistaken. Even more fundamentally the consultant recommended that the Council withdraw from the scheme of representation. The homes made no contribution to the Council's own need and representation was unnecessary.

## 3  PREMISES

The local authority can often help by the provision of premises, especially when these are temporarily surplus to requirements or being held pending commencement of a larger scheme of development. Such premises are cheap and can provide a great boost to a voluntary organisation on a short term basis. They can also be used to create provision in an area where there is a perceived need. The premises should be charged out at a proper rent, or the local authority will distort its knowledge of the provision it is making. As a facilitator, the local authority can exercise influence in its planning powers to secure community gain.

## 4  EQUIPMENT

In general voluntary organisation should be able to buy necessary equipment out of their own funds. In some cases, though, one off grants may be necessary for particularly expensive pieces of equipment of a capital nature (though often private trusts can help with non-recurring spending of this sort). In other cases expensive provision cannot be justified for one organisation only, but if held by the local authority could be made available to a number of organisations.

Kurz-Weill reading machines or deaf telephones are examples. They can be located in libraries but publicised through the voluntary organisations which can enable their participants to use them. In other cases voluntary organisations may rely upon services which the local authority can provide, e.g. a regular supply of talking books. More prosaically, local authorities might make available to voluntary organisations furniture and office equipment no longer required but still in reasonable condition.

## 5  TRAINING

The local authority often has facilities for training and organises training courses which can be extremely valuable to voluntary organisations. The council will regularly run, for example, management courses. Some of the larger voluntary organisations may well benefit from the opportunity to send staff on these courses. Demand may even justify the provision of special courses. These will benefit not only the organisation itself but also the council by making more cost effective use of the council's input and putting stress on the areas where the local authority wishes to expand services or change the organisation's direction. Local authorities traditionally neglect their own colleges of further education as a source for internal training. These can be encouraged to lay on courses not only for the local authority's own staff but also for the voluntary organisations in the borough. A typical college of further education will have a range of expertise which can make a major contribution to the expertise of volunteers.

## 6   ADVICE

In some cases the local authority can help organisations effectively by giving access to its range of professional services, e.g. the furnishing of advice – legal, financial, personnel or architectural. It is clearly important that such advice should not create dependency. It is usually possible to distinguish between the informal advice necessary to put an organisation on the right track and the formal when, for example, litigation has ensued. Clearly a local authority should not stand by and see an organisation it supports blunder into difficulty. This advice can also be used to prompt provision in the areas the authority wishes to see developed.

## 7   FUND RAISING

Apart from directing resources of its own to the voluntary organisation, the local authority can help it in fund-raising in several different ways. It can provide a focus for European Community social funding, which the organisation itself is unlikely to be able to reach. The local authority can play a part in the development of a community trust, through which local giving can be channelled to small local beneficiaries in particular. Private donors can include companies, fund raising groups like Rotary, Chambers of Commerce, etc. Solicitors can be encouraged to suggest community trusts to clients making wills. The potential can be substantial: the Secretary of the Thamesdown Community Trust has this advice for future community trusts:

> Give examples of actual projects – a company likes to know where its money is going.
> Make full use of contacts in business – a 'Mr Fixit' can be enormously helpful.
> Remember that the Trust matters to the voluntary sector as well – if they are hostile the Trust will go nowhere.
> Involve the voluntary sector at all stages, and include them on the Board of Trustees.
> Gear the grant giving policy to the needs.
> Fully research the local firms – find out their interests, who makes the decision, etc.
> Ask existing donors to give personal recommendations.
> Cold mail-shots do not yield results – ask for face-to-face interviews.
> Produce a statement of intent, illustrating the areas of involvement.
> Emphasise the fact that you are offering a service, and maximising their resources in the process.
> Be informed about the tax concessions, covenant procedure, present administration costs for the Trust, etc.
> Do not be seduced by the big names.
> Literature must look professional, but not glossy; ask companies and local colleges of art for design and printing. (*Community Trust Handbook 1987*).

The local authority can encourage payroll giving amongst its own employees and the employees of others – particularly through a community trust which can encourage local charities. It can play a pro-active role by reorganising its local charities where some are moribund. It is specifically empowered under the Charities Act 1960 to publish a local directory of charities which voluntary organisations can approach. It can encourage self help by voluntary organisations by promising matching funding, pound for pound, with money procured from elsewhere. The mayor can promote local charities not only by the traditional Christmas appeal but also by organising galas in local arts institutions, preferably sponsored by local enterprises and blessed by a fund raising committee. Such fund-raising may be general, but can also be used by the authority to prompt provision in specified areas by appropriate targetting of the appeal.

## Conclusion

The encouragement of community involvement is a good in itself, particularly where the deprived or handicapped are active protagonists in provision. Moreover such provision can enlarge greatly the statutory services which will never be able totally to meet need.

However substantial sums are now injected into voluntary organisations. These bodies are no more immune from the requirement to provide value for money than the local authority's own services. The council must therefore ensure that it receives value for money, by being clear in its aims and monitoring the output of the organisations. It must do so without being oppressive or dominating.

Positive actions can maximise the benefits from voluntary organisations. The council can make a variety of inputs which can aid the effectiveness and influence the direction of the organisation, of which cash is only one part.

### Using this chapter

▲   *Is your council fully aware of the benefits which may accrue from the systematic use of voluntary organisations to augment its own services and to enlarge choice to those in need in its area?*

▲   *Is your use of voluntary organisations such as to maximise the benefits they can offer? Do you take active steps to avoid problems?*

▲   *Is your council clear in its aims towards the voluntary sector? Are these clearly specified to the organisations? Where large sums of money are involved, do you specify the outputs required? Do you actively take steps to monitor the performance of the organisations?*

▲   *Do you take the opportunity of contributions to voluntary organisations to promote other council policies?*

▲   *Are you clear about the amount of money your council gives to the voluntary sector? And to each organisation? Is there a central register or organisation for dispensation of grants? Do you avoid hidden subsidies? (1)*

▲   *Does your giving enhance the freedom of the organisations? Or restrict it artificially by the giving of support in kind? Have you explored the value of short or long term secondments of local authority staff to organisations? (2)*

▲   *Do you make sure that you maximise the use of temporarily vacant premises (especially in areas of need) by making them available to voluntary organisations? (3)*

▲   *Do you provide access to specialised equipment which voluntary organisations themselves cannot afford? (4)*

▲   *Do you have a programme of targetted training for voluntary organisation staff and volunteers? Do you include the staff of voluntary organisations on the authority's own training courses or those provided by its college of further education?* (5)

▲ *Do you provide a ready channel for informal advice to voluntary organisations – without creating dependency?* (6)

▲ *Do you help voluntary organisations in their fund raising? What steps can you take to do so? Is your Council's aid to fund-raising targetted at areas of need?* (7)

# 9 Regulatory: influence by compulsion

## Key points

▲ The Council's regulatory functions can play a key part in an overall strategy
▲ Organisation structures and resourcing mechanisms must permit the prioritisation and targetting of regulatory functions
▲ The local authority must be able to exercise policy control or geographical discrimination within its regulatory services
▲ Public reaction is an important barometer of the effectiveness of the targetting of the regulatory function
▲ Where statutory powers are inadequate to meet need, it may be possible to change them
▲ In key areas regulatory services should be geared to joint work with other enforcement agencies
▲ The regulatory services can be a springboard to promotion of extra benefits to the council's overall strategies

## The local authority's regulatory powers

Local authorities are charged with a vast panoply of licensing, enforcement and regulatory functions. They spring from national legislation, local legislation and bye-laws. For some forgotten Victorian statutes, enforcement has long since ceased as being inappropriate to modern times. In other cases enforcement action is taken unenthusiastically on complaint only, like enforcement of the Sunday trading laws. In other cases there is rigid and automatic enforcement if a breach comes to light. Often the amount of enforcement activity depends upon the success of professional officers in securing resources from their local authorities. In many cases the enforcement capacity is selective in meeting demand which can be almost unlimited.

In most local authorities the regulatory function is not seen as an area which has any connection with the local authority's policies. It is part of a general backcloth to securing an acceptable quality of life. At estimate time the Trading Standards Officer or the Chief Environmental Health Officer will bid for more enforcement resources, citing the infrequency of inspections as justification. In other cases inadequacies may be thrown into sharp relief by a tragedy like a death by fire in a house in multiple occupation which has gone without inspection for some time. In taking the regulatory function for granted members often delegate decision taking (quite properly) to chief officers. At most they may be presented with a schedule showing prosecutions undertaken, warnings issued and success rate. Even those authorities looking at measurement of output can be confused on the effectiveness of their policies. Is a nil return, for example, evidence of total success? Or simply of inadequate enforcement? Do those authorities which wrest every ounce of benefit from a Section 52 Agreement with developers give the necessary resources to ensuring that the benefits are realised?

A substantial body of inspectors carry out the authority's functions of licensing, enforcement and regulation. There are also other inspectors whose job is not to identify matters for enforcement. They are there to check for dangerous paving stones, satisfactory reinstatements of road surfaces, empty premises for rating purposes, etc. In total this army of inspectors represents a formidable tool in the hands of the local authority. They constitute eyes and ears, with an intimate knowledge of the authority's area and its problems. Too often rigid professional boundaries prevent them from making a full contribution to the authority's knowledge.

## Regulation and the Council's strategy

The enforcement capability of a Council can make a substantial contribution to an authority's overall strategy. The contribution should not be allowed to go by default. While there is a common sense minimum below which certain enforcement functions should not be allowed to drop, nevertheless most regulatory capacity is distributed according to the value judgments of professional officers. This is not a necessary or desirable state of affairs. Discretion in the prioritisation and targetting of the regulatory function can be used so as to complement an authority's policy directives. While it is important that there should be fairness of policy within each category of enforcement, there can be discrimination in the use of resources both in terms of types of enforcement and geographical area. A total review of an authority's strategy in a specific sector will readily disclose which regulatory activities can contribute. Local authorities already make use of this capacity. The following are examples.

### PROTECTION OF LOCAL TRADE

One of the arguments mounted for retention of the Metropolitan Counties' Trading Standards operations, after the demise of their parent authorities, was the specialisation each of the organisations had built up. In itself this specialisation demonstrates how targetting of enforcement is possible. The trading standards organisations concentrated on problems besetting their local industries. In West Yorkshire, where the beleaguered textile industry was hit by foreign competition, major efforts were devoted to ensuring that competition was fair. In a trade where false labelling is extremely difficult to spot by the consumer, trading standards officers were able successfully to prosecute. The department was able to specialise in the wrongful attribution of foreign made textiles and garments to UK companies. Other trading standards operations looked to West Yorkshire as a centre of excellence on the topic. In the West Midlands, analagously, there was concentration on the motor trade. The department there became nationally reputed for its activities for the illegal clocking (i.e. turning back) of car odometers.

## TOURISM

Food premises play a major role in providing services to tourists. A bad experience can discredit and hamper a town's tourist efforts. Even more importantly, the fear of a bad experience can put tourists off. It is possible to use the inspection of food premises as a positive weapon in promoting tourism. The Bradford curry trail is a good example. Health inspectors frank the cleanliness of Asian restaurants, leaving the customer to validate the gastronomy. Westminster's clean caterers scheme fulfills a similar role. Westminster also maintains strong vigilance against unauthorised street traders – partly to protect legitimate traders but also to safeguard tourists against rip-offs. Seaside towns devote similar resources to mock auctions.

## THE ENVIRONMENT

In a city beset by litter, Westminster has introduced new local legislation, with an on the spot ticket for litter dropping and sixty inspectors charged with the job of watching for offenders. With the same bid to keep streets clean, a new bye-law produces a fine for owners of dogs who do not remove canine faeces when deposited on the street. Inspectors are charged with monitoring fly posting: offenders may be difficult to track, but if (as so often happens) the posters advertise organisations dealing with the Council, then alternative retribution may be possible. In an urban environment, the ability to telephone the Westminster noisy party patrol can bring instant relief and produce a disproportionate amount of good-will for the Council. Originally ending at 2 am, successive Notting Hill Carnivals have persuaded the Council to extend it till 6 am.

## HOUSING

In an authority like Westminster, where housing is at a premium, any housing loss or diminution in quality of life for its residents is a serious matter. As well as more direct steps to promote home ownership, the Council is prepared to purchase compulsorily housing which is not being properly used. In striving to maintain a uniquely high proportion of privately rented accommodation, the Council is active in ensuring standards by serving appropriate notices and by doing works in default. A special preoccupation is directed towards enforcement action to discontinue unlawful holiday lets. Particularly lucrative in the centre of London, such unauthorised uses diminish further the stock of housing for residents.

# How to target your Council's enforcement activities

## 1 DEPLOYMENT OF RESOURCES

The fragmentation of the enforcement services across professional boundaries makes flexible deployment of resources in the average local authority difficult. If there are two inspectors devoted to seeking out unauthorised skips, then it is difficult to redeploy them to a major drive on cracked paving stones or illegal scaffolding. The City of Westminster, in examining this problem, found that the authority employed 450 inspectors located in 29 different inspectorates. Analysis showed that they fell into three categories:

▽    public control, i.e. conforming to standards;
▽    service maintenance, i.e. checking the standard of Westminster's services
     such as street cleansing; and
▽    incidental service, i.e. facilitating a process such as the collection of rates.

Each of the inspectorates had different information systems. Sub-divisions of the City for inspection purposes were complex and varied. Not surprisingly some team areas were based on volume of work rather than geographical area. There were various other criteria for the sub-division of inspection areas. The Council regrouped its inspectorate into three:

▽    General highways inspectorate for:
     refuse enforcement
     street trading
     rates inspection
     parking meters
     Respark enforcement
     control of builders on highways
     emergency patrols
     street watch inspections
     skip inspections
     enforcement officers
▽    Environmental health inspectorate for:
     pest control
     residential inspection
     pollution, emergencies, etc
     entertainments licensing
     sex establishment licensing
▽    Building construction inspectorate for:
     drains in new buildings and large alterations
     building regulations

Information systems were integrated and the City sub-divided by common boundaries. Apart from the organisational advantages and the increased comprehensibility to the public, a major plus of the new system is the ability to redirect resources simply, without organisational change and without stepping on professional toes. Enforcement still remains in the hands of the basic departments to whom the inspectorates report. The potential of the system can ultimately extend to the use of expert systems which can in straightforward cases give inspectors an immediate enforcement capacity: portable computers can, for example, issue instant notices.

A similar multi-functional approach is being considered in Christchurch, which plans community wardens who will be the local authority contact with the public and check the quality of services delivered by contractors.

## 2   PRIORITISATION

A considerable amount of activity is demand led, that is to say inspectors respond to complaints from the public. There remains, however, a large body of routine inspections to a defined programme. This programme will stem from some sort of risk analysis. This may be the subjective view of the professional head as to what is required, or it may be a more sophisticated method based on statistical analysis. Most public health departments will, for example, inspect food premises known to have a bad record more frequently than those known to be exemplary in their hygiene. A modern computerised system may well be used to programme inspections according to this analysis.

Of course professional judgment will continue to play a major part in the level of enforcement activity. But there is no reason why members should not be aware of the priorities assumed by the department and should not have an input. The Council's own policy priorities can be used to influence the prioritisation of the inspectorates. If unauthorised street trading is, for example, a major concern, then the Council committee should be able to specify the relative proportion of resources allocated to it.

## 3   GEOGRAPHICAL CONCENTRATION

It should be possible for a council positively to discriminate in its enforcement activities towards distinct geographical areas. Certain areas are particularly prone to certain problems. The inspectorates will already take implicit account of this. A sex licensing operation in Westminster is likely to concentrate on Soho. Unlawful street trading is most likely to take place in the West End. Other needs may be less obvious. Members should be able to influence response to them. Geographical concentration of effort should span inspectorates, for problems are often multi-faceted. The Westminster Zone Improvement Patrol (ZIP) Team provides multi-inspectorate attention to one area of the City at a time, with appropriate publicity to maximise benefits.

## 4   USE OF THE PUBLIC

If the inspectors are the eyes and ears of the Council, then the public are more so. In deciding on its priorities, local authorities should have regard to the volume of complaints from residents. These provide a ready touchstone for the effectiveness of the enforcement function as well as the Council's services. Councils can monitor complaints by distributing reply paid post cards returned to a standard point, where they can be analysed. Complaints received separately by departments can be notified to the central point. An overwhelming concentration of complaints in one area will prompt the Council to prioritise on that service. In an area like Westminster, where licensing is extremely sensitive, a simple leaflet outlining procedures will help residents to have confidence to put forward their point of view. A Westminster Council leaflet for residents says:

> Most licence applicants are anxious to co-operate with local residents. A council officer will mediate between the applicant and the objectors by discussing with the applicant exactly what his intentions are, and what steps he can take to meet the residents' concerns.

About the hearing the leaflet says:

By law the Councillors on the sub-committee have to act impartially. They realise that often local residents have no experience of public speaking and are therefore given every assistance. Council officers, who are also impartial, will advise residents on points of procedure before the hearing starts.

Such documents – and such sensitiveness to public concerns – not only ensure that the Council's enforcement activities are related to perceived need, but also are excellent public relations in themselves.

## 5   IS THE LAW ADEQUATE?

If, in considering its sector strategy, a Council believes that the law is inadequate to meet needs, then it is always possible to change it. If, of course, this requires public general legislation, then the Council will need to mount a long and sustained campaign to win the hearts and the minds of Central Government. Even having done that the department may itself have a long wait before being allocated Parliamentary time. But there are alternatives. A local bill can be promoted. Local government has a long history of the promotion of local bills. While Government may not like idiosyncratic local provision, convincing evidence for the local problem may win Government support. Even more plausibly, if an experimental means of overcoming a national problem is canvassed, Government may be prepared to see a local pilot to assess likely success as a precursor for general legislation. Thus the City of Westminster has introduced private bills on litter and sex establishment licensing to strengthen its enforcement powers.

It may also be possible to change or bring in new bye-laws. Thus the City of Westminster's new bye-law penalising dog owners for failure to remove dog faeces from the street. Similar bye-laws in four other authorities make similar provision for canine faeces in parks. All are regarded by the Home Office as pilots which may prompt wider provision. In some cases it may be possible to take over services from an alternative enforcement agency. Thus the London Boroughs Association and the Association of London Authorities sunk their political differences to join in a common campaign to take over aspects of parking enforcement from the Metropolitan Police, complaining that the latter afforded enforcement low priority. The boroughs, beset by residents denied adequate parking space, were very anxious to step up enforcement.

## 6   JOINT WORKING WITH OTHER AGENCIES

In some cases enforcement problems transcend organisational boundaries. In looking at sex licensing and inspection of houses in multiple occupation, the police and fire services have a close involvement. Both share the same pre-occupations as the local authority and are very willing to co-operate. This joint working ensures that the complete range of statutory powers is available simultaneously in relation to any one premise. Joint working enables the organisations to share data and more effectively to target their joint enforcement activities. If one set of statutory powers are not relevant, another agency can use its own capabilities; or all powers can be used simultaneously to secure maximum effectiveness.

## 7   SELF REGULATION AND SIDE EFFECTS

The statutory enforcement activities can spawn self regulatory activities which may be even more effective in promoting the authority's goals. The Bradford curry trail and the Westminster clean catering scheme are examples. Not only do such extensions of statutory powers make the statutory powers more acceptable, but they also promote a positive contribution to the authority's goals. If fees are taken from licensees or putative licensees, some benefits (beyond statutory endorsement) can be conferred: thus the City of Westminster is launching a Theatreland project to broadcast the attractions of its theatres as some recompense for the substantial licensing fees which perforce it charges as part of its licensing role.

# Conclusion

The Council's enforcement and regulatory powers can be major elements in strategy implementation. They are capable of targetting to priority sectors or geographical areas provided that the organisation structure permits. Public reaction through analysis of complaints can provide a key pointer to the effectiveness of the function. Inadequate powers can be strengthened by changes in the law.

## Using this chapter

▲   *How can the regulatory functions assist the forwarding of the Council's policy objectives? Does your Council consciously prioritise enforcement activities in key areas? Are your Council's inspectorate teams able to communicate up the organisation so as to make it aware of the problems they encounter?*

▲   *Does your Council's organisation structure permit ready switching of priorities between enforcement activities? (1)*

▲   *Is there a policy input to the prioritisation of enforcement activities? Are the proportions of time devoted to non-demand led regulatory functions specified by the Council? (2)*

▲   *Do your Council's enforcement priorities discriminate toward certain geographical areas for certain functions? Is that a conscious decision of the Council? (3)*

▲   *Does your Council use the level of public complaints as an indicator by which it can target resources for enforcement matters? Does your Council analyse complaints in order to assess the areas of greatest public concern? (4)*

▲   *If your legal powers are inadequate, have you considered taking steps to change them? (5)*

▲   *In key areas do your enforcement teams work jointly and share data with other agencies? (6)*

▲   *Have you considered what spin-offs your enforcement activities can have for self help, public relations and promoting the Council's objectives? (7)*

# 10   The capacity to influence

## Key points

▲ *Every local authority seeks to influence the public and organisations which are in no way dependent upon it*
▲ *Public relations are of paramount importance; the support of the public is the local authority's most important asset*
▲ *In exercising influence, the local authority can create communities of interest, appeal to altruism and confer kudos*
▲ *Changes in service delivery can be influential*
▲ *Targeted advocacy can be effective*
▲ *Appeals to the courts may not win friends but can influence people*

## The need of the local authority to influence

A local authority looking at a total strategy for its area will soon be brought up short against the boundaries of its own functions. The previous chapters have contemplated situations where an external agency is in some way dependent on the local authority. The public perceives no such dependency in framing its own attitudes and behaviour. Most external agencies are not Council contractors or partners, receive no Council support and are oblivious to the effect the Council's regulatory powers might have on them. Many organisations perceive autonomy as a goal in itself: they avoid dependence. The organisational boundaries of public agencies usually follow professional boundaries which increase difficulties in forming common objectives. Organisations which are dependent on the local authority in one dimension may prize their independence in another. Organisations as varied as the Countryside Commission, the Training Agency and the Confederation of British Industry may see themselves as having an independent pressure group role. The private sector generally functions outside the direct ambit of the local authority. Both the concerns of residents and their ultimate welfare may depend on agencies with which the local authority has no self evident links.

## Public relations

Public relations means relations with the public. If a resident's direct experience with his local authority is unsatisfactory, then he is less likely to be sympathetic to the Council's aims in changing attitudes or behaviour. Getting closer to the customer has rightly become a major preoccupation of local authorities, spurred on by the Government's determination to give consumers an alternative route to services hitherto a local authority monopoly.

Communicating in order to exert influence is a skilled art. The co-operation of the media is essential. It is essential to find a figure head who is able to talk in simple language and create an impression of trustworthiness. The campaign must generate attractive headlines. It is vital to be in first with the communication. Personalised examples and memorable photographs capture media attention.

In procuring publicity, a local authority is now restricted by the Local Government Act 1986 as amended by the Local Government Act 1988. Its powers are in general limited to the provision of information on local government functions and services. The publicity must not appear to be designed to affect support for a political party. The test for the latter also includes whether the publicity promotes or opposes a point of view on a question of political controversy which is identifiable as a view of one political party and not of another. Councils must have regard to a code of practice promulgated by the Secretary of State for the Environment. Expenditure on publicity must be recorded in a separate account.

The effect of the Acts tends to be over-stated by local government. They do not represent a substantial inhibition of normal local authority publicity, though involvement of a lawyer at an early stage has now become vital. There is usually some nexus between any campaign and a local authority's statutory functions. Information, if appropriately presented, is difficult to distinguish from advocacy. There is, of course, in any event no bar on Councillors appearing on television or making statements to the media in their individual capacity, nor of political parties issuing press releases at their own expense. Properly advised, most Councils should be able to undertake public relations campaigns of all normal kinds.

Sometimes, of course, a Council will take a public stance because that is politically attractive or, indeed, necessary. It does not follow that it hopes to win the day. If, though, there is a clear intention to change public behaviour or the actions of an external agency, then a carefully planned campaign is necessary.

## Influencing outside organisations

There is usually available to any local authority only a limited amount of organisational energy capable of functioning at the boundaries of the organisation. Even in the ultimate enabling authority most time and effort will be committed to functions within the aegis of the Council. A local authority which wishes to extend its influence to outside organisations must organise itself accordingly.

Since its area is full of such organisations, it must prioritise those which are key to its strategy. It must devote itself only to those which are important in relation to the Council's objectives. The creation of forums with representative bodies is a straightforward step. Local authorities have a statutory duty to consult with businesses on their rate fixing. The introduction of the national non-domestic rate has changed the nature of those consultations: there will be a different community of interest, with business attempting to influence the provision of service by the local authority and the local authority, in turn, trying to influence the behaviour of business. Chambers of Commerce, Trade Associations and pressure groups generally all have a vested interest in maintaining a dialogue with the local authority. Such activities are part of the justification for their existence.

> The City of Westminster has promoted the Coach Working Party, an officer level forum to discuss coach issues in London, serviced and chaired by the Council. The coach and tourist industries participate with other London Boroughs, the Department of Transport, and the Police. Coach routeing and parking is a major problem to Westminster. The Council itself has produced a variety of traffic management and regulatory measures to control coaches. It has also provided off-street coach parking and coach meter spaces. The Coach Working Party has served to provide a code of practice acceptable to the industry, with summaries available in French and German. It has supervised the production of parking and other information for operators and drivers by the introduction of a coach parking card and a coach helper scheme to aid drivers with information on parking and routeing.

Without the co-operation of a representative body from the industry, such measures would not have been possible. Even so their effectiveness is limited. Not all operators belong to the Bus and Coach Council. Foreign operators certainly do not. Even those who do may not impose the code on their drivers and the ultimate decision taker is the driver himself. Representative bodies are of great importance through liaison machinery, but there is no substitute for direct access to decision takers.

This is obviously a particular problem where decision takers are at the operational level like coach drivers. If, conversely, decision takers are strategic, access may be limited by pressures on their time or, even more relevantly to many English local authorities, geographical distance. The local manager may not have the discretion sought by the local authority. It is clearly important for any Council to identify where the decisions vital to it are taken and target that decision taker.

## The Government and the European Commission

Influencing the European Commission is an art form in itself. Influencing the British Government is a no less complex matter, but without some of the arcana surrounding Brussels. Substantial organisations are dedicated to both tasks. A local authority will normally have access to one at least. If a local authority's need is part of a general case, then there should be no substantial benefit in separate action unless a special case can be proven. In many areas, though, the Council is seeking special treatment for funding for a project unique to its area. A Member of Parliament either at Strasbourg or Westminster will normally act as guide and interlocutor. Alternatively or in addition specialised firms of lobbyists can be employed. The function of the latter should not be misunderstood. They are procurers, intermediaries and information gatherers, not prime movers. That role must remain with the Council's members and officers.

## Means of influence

### 1   COMMUNITY OF INTEREST

Some external organisations have a natural community of interest with the local authority, while maintaining independence. The police and fire services are obvious examples. Chambers of Commerce and pressure groups are often at one with the local authority on many issues, if at odds on others. The organisations perceive their interdependence with the local authority. Such interdependence creates the opportunity for bargaining. Both sides expect benefits in a system described by the French as *chantage*. While this could be uncharitably translated as blackmail, it nevertheless performs a lubrication without which mutual machinery would not operate.

In less obvious areas it may be possible for the local authority to create a perception of community of interest. The adoption by the private sector of the Westminster Rescard results from the perception of the card as a marketing tool. It may be possible for the local authority to underscore marketing opportunities to the private sector in order to augment or replace its own provision. For example, the private sector is acutely aware of the growing number of elderly, 25 % of whom live alone. Many of these are free from money cares but need services. This represents an opportunity to the private sector which could relieve local authorities of substantial statutory responsibilities. The CBI's task force on urban regeneration has pointed out that charity alone cannot halt the process of urban decay. If commercial decisions will be taken, then local authorities must make the private sector aware of commercial potential. Local authorities can also act as disseminators of information. Thus the Department of Trade and Industry actively employs local authorities, with their specialised knowledge of local businesses, to act as a spur to export drives. The Hertfordshire County Council publishes a series on economic trends and issues, the main aim of which is to alert local businesses to the possibilities available to them. The County Council is working with the Hertfordshire Chamber of Commerce to establish an agency to provide information on the harmonised single European market. Knowledge of European codes of practice and standards will be key to the expansion or, indeed, survival of UK businesses. The Hertfordshire slogan is: 'L'Europ c'est un marché de l'avenir, mais il faut s'y préparer immédiatement'. The same bulletin heightens the message by picking out the implications of the Channel Tunnel, bringing 90 million people within 250 miles of Hertfordshire and leaving Lille as close as Leeds or Manchester.

A community of interest extends beyond an immediate financial benefit. The private sector perceived a long-term need to link with the education system to ensure a supply of suitable employees – hence the highly successful London Education Business Partnership. Business will often perceive problems caused by environmental damage arising from their industry. Generators of litter can often be persuaded to sponsor a litter bin outside their own premises.

The fast food industry in Westminster is a major producer of litter. It takes only 45 hamburger cartons to fill one of the City Council's 8000 litter bins. The Council held a fast food seminar at the start of a campaign to enlist the help of the industry itself in cleaning up the streets. Their aid was sought in sponsoring more bins, employing their own street sweepers, reviewing their product packaging and arousing public awareness of the litter problem. Because the public image of the companies was at stake, the campaign had a quick success.

Reputable operators will often subscribe to codes of practice partly because of the image of their industry but with the side benefit of making conspicuous the cowboys in their trade. The City of Westminster has agreed codes of practice with coach operators, despatch riders and exchange bureaux. If a long term operation, such codes put pressure on those who do not subscribe to meet industry-recognised standards.

## 2 PUBLIC SUPPORT

The most potent of all weapons in exerting influence is public support. Sometimes statutory services can do no more: public participation itself is the only means of securing an improvement. Thus the City of Westminster has become convinced that the only key to improving the condition of its streets is to make litter dropping as unsocial as spitting has now become. Public perception of expectoration as unhygienic and anti-social has almost banished it from the streets. Similar attitudes towards litter dropping, taking of drugs or precautions against AIDS – not to mention registration for community charge – would solve problems overnight. In creating this attitude the local authority has a number of assets. It has ready access to the media, has councillors who are local spokespersons, has locations for siting posters, machinery for distribution of civic newspapers and leaflets, numerous points of inter-action with the public and in some cases access to local channels on cable television. Not all local authorities have Westminster's One Stop Services points, but all have local offices and most importantly libraries, a greatly underused resource in the dissemination of information.

The distribution of facts and data through the Council's information points can be extremely effective. Milton Keynes has a Community Viewdata Service which gives thousands of pages of information about what is happening in and around Milton Keynes. Civic information is one of the many services obtainable. Voluntary groups can also rent space on the system. Free public terminals are available. Over thirty view data systems are already operated by local authorities. More than sixty make information available to the public using computerised systems. Expert systems are available or can be created to give user friendly access to a variety of information, including welfare rights, housing benefits and tenancy transfers.

In an era of consumer sovereignty influence can often be most effectively used in conjunction with consumer groups. Consultation and, even better, involvement of tenant management groups, parent/teacher associations and school governors can create a sense of proprietorship on their part as well as a closeness to the customer. Groups may be key to the local authority's concern. In seeking to exert influence through public relations, the local authority must be clear as to which public it means to influence. Different publics have different access points. The Greater London Council, for example, ran the biggest ever local authority campaign to defeat its abolition. The campaign won prizes and, it was claimed, influenced a substantial majority of Londoners to support the retention of the Council. If the Council's intentions were to defeat abolition, then the campaign was conspicuously unsuccessful. Indeed it stiffened the Government's sinews. If the intention was to defeat abolition then the campaign should have been targetted on the Government and not on the public.

If opinion-formers can be identified, then it is usually cost-effective to target a campaign specifically at them. It is much easier to pitch a campaign at a finite and clearly defined group of people. Thus the City of Westminster, in planning its takeover of education powers from the Inner London Education Authority, identified headteachers and teachers as key opinion-formers. The Council wished to reassure the public about the safety of entrusting education to its care. Alarmed teaching staff would spread concern to parents. A programme of face to face contacts with headteachers and teachers by councillors and the Chief Executive took away fear and uncertainty as to the future. Other client groups like the handicapped, the elderly and women are more diffuse – but each have clearly defined access points.

## 3   ALTRUISM

The most successful appeal to public spiritedness is the British Blood Transfusion Service. Countries which pay for blood have problems – in the amount of blood they can collect, the financial burden and, sometimes, the quality of blood. The perception of public good is a weapon which the local authority can use. Appeals for foster parents, 'adoption' of an elderly pensioner or a general appeal for volunteers can often produce motivated members of society who rejoice in the warm glow produced by their altruism.

## 4   KUDOS

The local authority can induce action by conferment of prestige. A visit by the Mayor, with newspaper photograph, may be enough to stimulate further efforts or emulation elsewhere. A Member of Parliament, a Minister of the Crown, or Lord Lieutenant may be procurable. At the top of the list comes a Royal visit. The local authority, directly or indirectly, is often in a better position to procure such endorsement than a private organisation. Such visits – not to mention conferment of honours – can be powerful motivators.

## 5   LAND AND INFRASTRUCTURE

Local authorities have a direct and obvious means of influencing decision taking by the private sector through making available land for appropriate purposes. Local authorities are major landowners and land represents a resource which can be applied towards a strategy. Zoning decisions in unitary plans are equally key to a strategy. The local authority has powers of compulsory land assembly. It can lay on the infrastructure which enables land to be developed. Planning briefs for major development opportunities will be a major factor in the provision made. Even if these might be difficult to defend on appeal, most developers (given the amount of cash tied up in a modern development) would prefer to work with a constructive planning authority rather than fight it to appeal. But a planning authority must remember its bargaining position. If it is desperate to attract the development then it cannot afford to be over-demanding or restrictive in its planning brief. Authorities where development opportunities are at a premium can be more choosy.

General infrastructure provision by the local authority may be relevant to outside agencies, particularly the private sector. A developer can be encouraged by the Council providing housing for key workers. Specialised vocational provision in Colleges of Further Education may well influence locational decisions. Matching of skills to job opportunities is becoming a major preoccupation for Councils which have job vacancies in their areas coupled with high unemployment.

Inadequate local authority services may also contribute to problems. For example, could inadequate educational provision cause unwanted outward migration of couples with school age children? Could traffic problems be caused by inadequate signing? Can sleeping policemen contribute to improving the environment on a housing estate?

Local authorities have become much more conscious of the influence of the general environment on the potential of their areas. Greening programmes are under way. Promotional literature stresses easy access to the countryside. Many local authorities are now committed to flagship arts projects, as much to improve the image of their area as for cultural reasons. Thus Council support for the City of Birmingham Symphony Orchestra, the Bradford Alhambra, the Sheffield Crucible, the Manchester Royal Exchange, the Royal Shakespeare Company season in Newcastle. Flagship projects like the National Exhibition Centre in Birmingham – not to mention attempts to secure international events for the area – play a part.

## 6   ADVOCACY

Advocacy is assumed as a role by every local authority. Unfortunately the dispassionate presentation of a case, however overwhelming, is rarely enough to guarantee success. The local authority has access to many networks. The key to success will be using these networks to identify and motivate the right allies: pressure groups, trade associations, trade unions, Members of Parliament. Often allies can be found within the targetted organisations, which often have a variety of interests. So in Government it may be possible to encounter an unsympathetic lead Ministry, but find allies in other departments. Cumulative pressure by colleagues can change departmental views. Access through the technostructure is often possible. There is, for example, an extremely close relationship between local authority professionals and their colleagues in Government Ministries. Sometimes these are extended through joint working over many years.

It is important to access the technostructure at the right level. Go too high and you may find an officer without detailed knowledge of the issue, without time to research it fully and therefore dependent on the brief given to him by his subordinate – perhaps the very person whose judgment you are trying to get overruled. Go too low and you may find an officer working strictly within departmental policy – the very policy which you seek to overturn. Direct appeal to Ministers by politicians is rarely successful unless the Civil Service have been briefed in advance. A pre-meeting or discussions by officials can establish the areas where concessions can be made if the right demands are formulated. If the local authority demands correlate to the Civil Servant's brief to Ministers, then a productive meeting becomes possible. Few Ministers have the time to devote to taking such issues beyond the brief provided to them by their Civil Servants. Such principles apply equally to negotiations with other organisations.

Councils should concentrate upon the achievable. They are highly unlikely, for example, to shift a Government manifesto commitment. But at the margin significant changes may be made. Thus general opposition to the abolition of the Metropolitan Counties or the introduction of the Community Charge was unsuccessful. But the campaign to keep police forces and fire brigades intact won ready support from the Home Office. The London Boroughs Association was successful in inducing a Government change of mind on the retention of residual rating. It succeeded not on grounds of principle but by stressing the managerial difficulties for London local authorities in running two systems simultaneously at a time when financial managers were already under acute pressure to implement Government changes. It is important to use the arguments that will appeal to the listener, not necessarily those which are uppermost in the minds of the Council. Barristers work on the same principle, often ignoring what their clients believe could be the principal argument in favour of those which can be projected satisfactorily in the court.

Occasionally publicity stunts may be effective. The Jarrow march captured the imagination of a nation. To exemplify problems caused by the closure of Westminster Hospital, the City of Westminster staged an ambulance race which gave the public and press a ready understanding of the issue. Epitomisation or personalisation of problems in this way can project the message.

## 7   THE COURTS

If all else fails, then litigation or the threat of litigation can be effective. Previous chapters have discussed the local authority's scope in judicial review and enforcement proceedings. But all organisations have to act within the general law. The London Boroughs Association, acting jointly with the Association of London Authorities, persuaded British Rail and London Regional Transport to introduce measures to prevent pigeons roosting on bridges over roads (causing heavy bills for cleaning droppings and compensation for slipping pedestrians). The undertakers avoided litigation by splitting the cost of netting the bridges. Derbyshire County Council has brought a prosecution against the North West Water Authority for putting sewage effluent illegally into the river Goyt. Data needed for the prosecution came from the water authority's own published material.

The threat of prosecution is often better than the deed itself. Local authorities will often need a long term relationship with the body concerned. A successful prosecution is hardly likely to cement relationships.

## Conclusion

Local authorities have the capacity to influence those who do not have a direct relationship with them. Often such influence may be key to a local authority's strategy. Changing public behaviour calls for a sustained and well thought through campaign. Public attitudes may be affected by a direct lobby on influence-formers.

Influencing outside organisations, including Government, can often succeed by identifying common areas of self interest or appropriate allies. The local authority's own functions may be key to a successful initiative. Changes in the delivery of services by the Council may influence the attitude of outside organisations.

### Using this chapter

▲   *In what areas does your Council's strategy require changes in behaviour by third parties? Have you clearly identified the agencies or publics which you wish to influence?*

▲   *Have you earmarked officers with specific responsibility for influencing key outside agencies? Do they have sufficient time to build up the necessary relationships?*

▲   *Does your public relations department play a key role in supporting the Council's strategy? Or does it merely churn out press releases on the Council's decisions?*

▲   *Can you identify a community of interest with external agencies? Can you point out to them commercial opportunities, which, if taken, will promote the Council's strategy? (1)*

▲   *In key areas, does your Council's strategy enjoy public support? Is your Council credible to its residents? Do they perceive it as their Council, working for them? (2)*

▲   *Have you appealed to public-spiritedness? (3)*

▲   *Does the Council procure recognition for those who help its objectives? (4)*

▲   *Can you change the delivery of your Council's services so as to promote strategy? Is the image of your area right? Are your planning powers used consciously to further the Council's strategy? (5)*

▲   *In your advocacy, do you concentrate on what is achievable? Do you earmark key allies? Are your Members of Parliament on your side? Have you made full use of the technostructure? (6)*

▲   *Do you monitor the activities of outside agencies in key areas to see whether prosecution or legal action (or its threat) can be effective in securing a change of policy? (7)*

# 11   Conclusion

The enabling authority is here to stay. The local authority's monopoly of direct supply of services is disappearing. The concept is increasingly attractive both to left and right. Arm's length agencies are being created as much by the initiative of local authorities as by Government legislation. A global megatrend may be at work. The Gibbs committee, in New Zealand, has proposed a tier of health authorities which will be statutorily prohibited from owning or managing any services. They would buy services from the best available source. UK local authority direct service organisations are saying the same thing about central support departments.

There is a long way to go before a local authority exits entirely from direct service provision, if indeed such a situation ever arises. Regulatory functions, for example, do not lend themselves easily to contracting out. Originally anathematised in the world of local government the concept of the enabling authority is nevertheless becoming increasingly attractive as its virtues are recognised. The Widdicombe Committee rejected the separation of the political from the executive by investing officers with separate statutory powers on the model of the Passenger Transport Authority/Passenger Transport Executive split. But the enabling authority will increasingly operate through executive agencies – public and private – with independent status.

The role of the local authority as a conduit for pluralism is not without irony. Historically public provision and choice have been seen as incompatible. The enabling authority will see its role as extending consumer choice. Some will claim that the Government has disabled the enabling council by its restrictions on finance and powers. Others will point out the exclusion of local government spending from the PESC totals, thus bringing it outside the formal aegis of Government concern. Certainly this is a move long sought by local government. The introduction of the national non-domestic rate and the community charge should also prompt Government to take a great deal less interest in the level of local government spending.

The enabling authority need not be less effective or influential than a local authority pre-occupied with providing services directly. It has substantial leverages not only on its contractors but on many other agencies with which it inter-relates. This book has described the various ways in which the local authority can use those leverages through different relationships so as to make an impact on the provision for its community. Without the incubus of the administration of a substantial direct service provision, time will be freed for a more strategic concentration of effort. As Councils become closer to their customers, they will become increasingly conscious of unmet needs. They will perceive as a key role protection of the consumer and the environment. As well as being a watchdog (especially on bodies immune from detailed public scrutiny) they will have a positive role to enable social and economic well-being in their areas. This role will call for a new type of local authority strategic planning. Taking a holistic view of their areas will prompt Councils to concentrate on key areas of need. Sectoral planning and concentration on specific client groups or geographical areas will underline local authorities' role as enablers and regulators. Resources will be better targeted towards need as concentration on the council's own services diminishes. Greater precision will be sought in control and regulation. Committee structures will be changed not only to reflect the client/contractor split but also to correspond to the larger preoccupation with overall welfare.

The traditional structure and role of local authority departments will also not necessarily be appropriate to the needs of the enabling authority. A local authority free from executive responsibility can restructure its departmental organisation more easily to correspond to its overall strategy. The professional base can disappear; indeed a professionally-oriented department may present that one-dimensional view which the local authority is anxious to reject in favour of a total approach. The Chief Executive is key to the change. Recognising that the nature of the local authority is changing, he must:

▽   ensure that the authority has in place the strategic planning capability needed for its new role;
▽   create a management structure related to key areas of strategy and flexible enough to respond to a changing environment;
▽   develop the outward-looking role so as to establish key external relationships and mechanisms;
▽   form structures for joint planning and implementation with other key agencies at different organisational levels.

As the skills of the Chief Executive must change, so must those of other officers. The shift towards an enabling authority is going to call for a major change in attitudes. The separation of the client and contractor role will polarise officers, with managerially inclined officers gravitating to the service organisations or contractors. The client roles will call for officers with a sense of strategy and political skills. A more entrepreneurial style will be essential. Energy must be concentrated at the boundaries of the organisation and not dissipated internally. The comfort of a large bureaucracy will be withdrawn. There will be a premium on innovative thinking and the ability to create new forms of partnership and joint working. Management in the enabling authority will be just as stimulating and, perhaps, more demanding than management in an old style direct service Council. The role of the catalyst in presenting opportunities to others presents a challenge to the officer. There is every sign that local government officers are moving to meet the challenge. Already considerable initiative has been shown in creating a wide variety of innovative provision – from restructuring direct labour organisations to management buy-outs, from introduction of local management in schools to the creation of enterprise boards, from setting up tenant co-operatives to forming new housing associations.

How will councillors adapt to the enabling authority? Those who have seen their role as running direct service provision and have enjoyed the administrative routine it brings will be disappointed. It will seem to them that their powers are being transferred to officers in one guise or another.

The administrative warp and woof of committee business will disappear, to be replaced by what? The answer must be a concentration on and an overview of a strategy for their area (which is what many commentators feel councillors should have been doing all the time). Members must concentrate on their role as watchdogs of the area's well-being. They must monitor the effectiveness of their policies by their impact on the external environment. They must assess performance – both of their own officers and of the agencies with which they work. They must develop indicators which alert them to significant changes in key areas of concern. They must preserve competition in the supply of services by safeguarding different providers. They must ensure that choice is available to all. Their overwhelming pre-occupation must be with objectives and performance.

This process will bring with it implications well beyond the scope of this book, especially when coupled with the far-reaching effects of the changes in local government finance. There will be a trend towards more direct charging. New forms of internal working will be devised within authorities. Small area data bases will be created. The constituency role of the member will be accentuated as the member seeks to use the authority's influence in provision in his constituency. Authorities will need fewer Councillors, but the rationale for large authorities will disappear with their exit from direct service provision.

The enabling authority of the future need not be ineffective. Its influence for the welfare of its people can be greater than that of the present local authority. But the management change implied must be firmly grasped. The mechanisms for enabling exist. Councillors and officers must be sure that they know how to work them.

# Select bibliography

Associations of County Councils, District Councils and Metropolitan Authorities (1988) *Stimulating Local Authority Enterprises – The Local Authority Role*.

Audit Commission (1986) *Making a Reality of Community Care*. HMSO.

Audit Commission (1988) *Competitive Management of Parks and Open Spaces*. HMSO.

Audit Commission (1989) *Preparing for Compulsory Competition*. HMSO.

Barratt, J. and Downs, J. (1988) *Organising for Local Government*. Longman.

Bennington, J. and Elliott, D. (1988) 'The Challenge of Change'. *Local Government Policy Making*. Vol. 15, No. 1.

Bogdanor, V. et al. (1988) *Against the Over-mighty State*. Federal Trust for Education and Research.

Brindley, T. and Stoker, G. (1988) 'Partnership in Inner City Urban Renewal'. *Local Government Policy Making*. Vol. 15, No. 2.

Brooke, R. (1988) 'English Local Government'. *The Administrator*. Sept. 1988.

Brooke, R. (1988) 'Towards a Stable Administration'. *Local Government Studies*. July/August 1988.

CBI Task Force on Business and Urban Regeneration (1988) *Initiatives Beyond Charity*.

Clarke, M., Brooke, R., Travers, T. et al. (1987) *Local Government and Business*. Municipal Journal.

Clarke, M. and Stewart, J. (1988) *The Enabling Council*. Local Government Training Board.

Community Trust Handbook (2nd edn) (1987) Community Trust Development Unit.

Department of the Environment (1988) *Local Authorities' Interests in Companies*. HMSO.

Department of the Environment (1988) *Tenant's Choice*. DoE.

Department of Health and Social Security and Welsh Office (1988) *Working Together*. HMSO.

Flynn, N. and Leach, S. (1984) *Joint Boards and Joint Committees*. INLOGOV.

Griffiths, Sir R. (1988) *Community Care: Agenda for Action*. HMSO.

Gutch, R. and Young, K. (1988) *Partners or Rivals?* Local Government Training Board.

HM Government (1988) *Action for Cities*. HM Government.

HM Government (1988) *Financing our Public Library Service*. HMSO.
*HM Government Response to the Report of the Widdicombe Committee of Inquiry (1988)*. HMSO.
Home Office (1987) *Report of the Working Group on Juvenile Crime*.
Leach, S. and Stewart, J. (1986) *The Conditions of Joint Action*. INLOGOV.
Leach, S., Vielba, C. and Flynn, N. (1987) *Two Tier Relationships in British Local Government*. INLOGOV.
Local Government Training Board (1987) *After Widdicombe*. LGTB.
Local Government Training Board (1988) *Councillors and Competition; Organising for Competition; The Client Role in Competition; Quality and Competition*. LGTB.
Local Government Training Board (1988) *Going for Better Management*. LGTB.
Local Government Training Board (1988) *Managing Tomorrow*. LGTB.
McKeganey, N. and Hunter, D. (1986) 'Only Connect . . .' *Policy and Politics*. Vol. 14, No. 3.
National Audit Office (1988) *Urban Development Corporations*. HMSO.
National Local Authority Forum on Drugs Misuse (1988) First Report.
Rhodes, R. (1988) *Beyond Westminster and Whitehall*. Unwin Hyman.
Ridley, N. (1988) *The Local Right*. Centre for Policy Studies.
SOLACE/NACRO (1987) *Local Authority Action on Juvenile Crime*.
SOLACE/LGTB (1988) *Managing Competition*. HMSO.
Stewart, J. (1986) *The New Management of Local Government*. Allen and Unwin.
Stewart, J. (1986) *The Management of Influence*. Local Government Training Board.
Stewart, J. (1988) *Understanding the Management of Local Government*. Longman.
Stewart, J. (1988) *A New Management for Housing Departments*. LGTB.
Stewart, J., Leach, S., Rhodes, R. et al. (1980) 'Interorganisational Relationships'. *Town Planning Review*. 51(3), July 1980.
Stewart, J. and Stoker, G. (1988) *From Local Administration to Community Government*. Fabian Society.
Stoker, G. (1988) *The Politics of Local Government*. Macmillan.
Stoker, G., Wedgewood Oppenheim, F. and Davis, M. (1988) *The Challenge of Change*. INLOGOV.
Widdicombe. *Report of the Committee of Inquiry into the Conduct of Local Authority Business (1986)*. HMSO.

# Index